CHILD CENTRED PLANNING IN THE EARLY YEARS FOUNDATION STAGE

Sara Miller McCune founded SAGE Publishing in 1965 to support the dissemination of usable knowledge and educate a global community. SAGE publishes more than 1000 journals and over 800 new books each year, spanning a wide range of subject areas. Our growing selection of library products includes archives, data, case studies and video. SAGE remains majority owned by our founder and after her lifetime will become owned by a charitable trust that secures the company's continued independence.

Los Angeles | London | New Delhi | Singapore | Washington DC | Melbourne

CHILD CENTRED PLANNING

IN THE EARLY YEARS FOUNDATION STAGE

JO MCEVOY & SAMANTHA MCMAHON

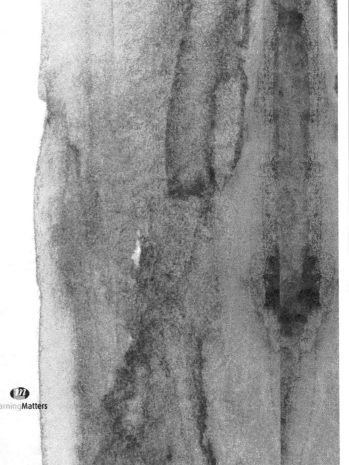

⑤SAGE | **LearningMatters**

Learning Matters
An imprint of SAGE Publications Ltd
1 Oliver's Yard
55 City Road
London EC1Y 1SP

SAGE Publications Inc.
2455 Teller Road
Thousand Oaks, California 91320

SAGE Publications India Pvt Ltd
B 1/I 1 Mohan Cooperative Industrial Area
Mathura Road
New Delhi 110 044

SAGE Publications Asia-Pacific Pte Ltd
3 Church Street
#10-04 Samsung Hub
Singapore 049483

Editor: Amy Thornton
Senior project editor: Chris Marke
Project management: Swales & Willis Ltd, Exeter, Devon
Marketing manager: Lorna Patkai
Cover design: Wendy Scott
Typeset by: C&M Digitals (P) Ltd, Chennai, India

Library of Congress number: 2019935710

British Library Cataloguing in Publication Data

A catalogue record for this book is available from the British Library

ISBN 978-1-5264-3912-3
ISBN 978-1-5264-3913-0 (pbk)

CONTENTS

ABOUT THE EDITORS AND CONTRIBUTORS

THE EDITORS

Jo McEvoy is the Subject Leader for Primary Education and EYTS at the University of Huddersfield. She has extensive experience of teaching, leadership and advisory work in the Early Years. She has previously worked as a deputy headteacher, local authority quality team leader, Early Years teacher and pre-school supervisor.

Samantha McMahon is a Subject Leader for Early Years at the University of Huddersfield with considerable experience of working with Early Years students and the sector. She has more than 20 years' experience of working with children and young people and is particularly interested in leadership in Early Years and children's physical development.

THE CONTRIBUTORS

Kate Banfield is a qualified, experienced and knowledgeable contributor to the Early Years and childcare profession. She has developed, led and managed high quality day care settings, training centres and children's centres. As a qualified adult teacher she has effectively written and delivered training to professionals and parents across a wide range of subjects and countries. She is an associate EYTS link tutor for Huddersfield University and is presently developing her own small kindergarten in Nanyuki, Kenya.

Amanda Crow is a Senior Lecturer and Early Years course leader at the University of Huddersfield. She is an experienced practitioner having previously worked in a variety of settings ranging from local authority day care provision to managing Sure Start Children's Centres. Amanda is passionate about enabling students to gain from both their academic and practical experiences, believing this combination is needed to ensure graduates are best equipped to support children in their Early Years settings.

Mary Dyer is the Subject Leader for the Undergraduate Framework in the School of Education and Professional Development at the University of Huddersfield. She has recently completed her Doctor of Education, investigating the professional identity and agency of graduate Early Years practitioners. Mary's work in Early Years includes establishing NVQ Assessment Centres in Childcare, Play Work, and Health and Social Care, and as a local authority Development Officer supporting Early Years settings in developing their provision and meeting Ofsted's inspection and registration requirements.

Nicola Firth is a Senior Lecturer in Early Years at the University of Huddersfield. She has worked in higher education for 12 years, working with students on under-graduate and postgraduate programmes. Prior to working in higher education Nicola worked in Early Years settings as a Nursery Nurse, then Nursery Manager.

Alison Ryan is a Senior Lecturer in the School of Education and Professional Development at the University of Huddersfield. Since joining the university in 2002 she has been responsible for teaching on a number of programmes across the school focusing on Literacy, Maths and Inclusive Learning. Alison's teaching career started in 1988. Her first role as a tutor for young people with learning difficulties and disabilities in a London Further Education college led to a subsequent career in Adult Education where she taught on and developed family learning programmes in partnership with the local authority.

Karen Smith works as a Senior Lecturer in Childhood Studies at the University of Huddersfield. Previously, Karen taught in primary education for 18 years before working for the local education authority as a principal officer. This role particularly focused on the private, voluntary and independent sectors with strategic responsibility for partnership working, inclusion and the development of information services for children and families. Karen returned to teaching as a teacher of Early Years at a sixth form college, prior to joining the university.

Kate Smith works as an associate link tutor on the University of Huddersfield Early Years Initial Teacher Training programme, mentoring, assessing and teaching students. Previously, she owned and managed a private day nursery. Kate developed and led the outstanding provision, providing a wealth of rich learning opportunities for children in a deprived inner city area. She has utilised her skills working as a freelance consultant to mentor other Early Years settings in the private, voluntary and independent sectors.

Angela Sugden works as a freelance Early Years consultant and is an associate link tutor for the University of Huddersfield Early Years Initial Teacher Training programme. Previously she worked in local authorities where she developed and led the Early Years provision on a trailblazer Sure Start local programme, one of the first five programmes in the country. Angela has also been an area early learning manager supporting practitioners and parents to provide the best possible early learning experiences for children from birth to five years.

Lindsey Watson is a Senior Lecturer in Early Childhood at the University of Huddersfield. Lindsey is currently studying for a Doctor of Philosophy with research focusing on 'What younger children really think and understand about internet safety: The value of stories and role play as research methods'.

ACKNOWLEDGEMENTS

We would like to express our gratitude to all the practitioners and managers who have helped in making this book through contributing to our focus group or allowing us to use examples of their practice in our case studies. Our thanks go to:

Sarah Bambury (EYT) – deputy nursery manager

Elizabeth Brooke (EYT) – deputy nursery manager

Miriam Caldercott (EYT) – EYFS lead/reception class teacher

Clare Cawthra (EYT) – deputy pre-school leader

Samantha Clarke – trainee Early Years Teacher

Sarah Collins (EYT) – pre-school Early Years Teacher

Claire Jackson (QTS) – pre-school manager

Bethany Ley – undergraduate student, BA Hons Early Years

Melissa Lumb (EYT) – nursery manager

Chloe Marsden (EYT) – nursery deputy manager

Felicity Sutcliffe (EYT) – pre-school manager

Dawn Trucca (QTS, EYP) – reception class teacher

Emma Turner (EYT) – nursery class teacher

Ashlea Wall – undergraduate student, BA Hons Early Years

Manager and staff at Rainbows Nursery, Salford

SECTION 1

OVERVIEW OF PLANNING IN THE EARLY YEARS FOUNDATION STAGE

1 THE PLANNING CONTEXT

Jo McEvoy

CHAPTER AIMS

By the end of this chapter you will be able to:

- understand the background and context from which the Early Years Foundation Stage (EYFS) has evolved
- explain and make appropriate use of the statutory and non-statutory documents that make up the EYFS framework
- describe the underpinning knowledge and skills that are required for curriculum planning in the EYFS
- appreciate that the context in which you work will influence your decisions about how you plan for learning in the EYFS

As you read this chapter, refer to pages 1–5 of *Development Matters in the Early Years Foundation Stage (EYFS)* (Early Education, 2012).

INTRODUCTION

Planning for learning in the Early Years Foundation Stage (EYFS) is not a simple task. It requires you to understand and apply the principles of the *EYFS Statutory Framework* (DfE, 2017, p6), know and understand the learning needs of your children and appreciate the particular context in which you work. There is no easy 'one size fits all' solution, because planning in the EYFS requires you to make decisions based on sound professional judgement and understanding of child development theory. Therefore, it is often the case that planning can be perceived as a daunting task, taking up hours of time and not always achieving its intended outcomes. It is easy to fall into the trap of planning for activities and topics, rather than planning for learning. While these activities and topics may be enjoyable and educational, there is the danger that without giving sufficient attention to the learning that you want children to experience, the learning potential and progress of some children may be compromised.

Therefore, this chapter aims to set the scene for the whole of this book by exploring the wider context for planning in the EYFS. It will guide you through the statutory and non-statutory guidance for the EYFS, so that you can become more confident in making professional, informed decisions about how you plan for children's learning and development. It will support you to use the non-statutory guidance, *Development Matters in the Early Years Foundation Stage* (Early Education, 2012) appropriately, as an assessment tool to support child-centred planning that takes into account child development theory and the characteristics of effective learning and teaching. At the heart of this chapter and throughout this book is the key message that planning should not be a paper exercise, but rather, the means through which you ensure that all children make progress because you are responsive to their individual needs and you capitalise on learning opportunities as they arise.

THE EARLY YEARS FOUNDATION STAGE: BACKGROUND AND CONTEXT

The current version of the EYFS framework (DfE, 2017) has evolved from the original EYFS that was produced in 2007 and became statutory in 2008. It was an integral part of the Every Child Matters agenda (DfES, 2004) that sought to integrate children's services to work together towards the achievement of five outcomes incorporating education, health and well-being. The policy context surrounding the original version of the EYFS was focused on closing the gap in outcomes between children from disadvantaged and non-disadvantaged backgrounds. There was a drive to raise the quality and increase sufficiency of childcare and early education for the achievement of two aims. First, ensuring sufficient childcare to enable parents to continue working was part of the drive to reduce child poverty and second, raising the quality of child care and early education was the means to securing positive outcomes for all children and particularly for those from disadvantaged backgrounds. Four themes with accompanying principles underpinned the original EYFS. These were: the Unique Child, Positive Relationships, Enabling Environments and Learning and Development (DCSF, 2008) and although there have since been three subsequent revisions to the EYFS (DfE, 2012, 2014, 2017), it is important to note that these underpinning themes have remained the same.

TICKELL'S REVIEW OF THE EYFS

The first revision to the original EYFS was undertaken in 2011 by Dame Tickell (Tickell, 2011). The review had been planned since the EYFS was first introduced in order to evaluate the effectiveness of this new integrated approach to care and education for children from birth to five years. Tickell consulted widely with stakeholders about how useful the EYFS framework was in practice and its success in meeting its aims. She made 46 recommendations, some of which have influenced how practitioners assess and plan for learning today. Practitioners reported that assessment processes using the original version of the EYFS were cumbersome and required too much paperwork. They were concerned that this was taking them away from time spent interacting with and teaching children. Although Tickell acknowledged that excessive recording of assessments was an inaccurate interpretation of the EYFS statutory requirements, she did advise on a slimming down of the EYFS and made recommendations for simplifying assessment, reducing the number of Early Learning Goals to 17 and insisting that 'paperwork should be kept to the absolute minimum required to promote children's successful learning and development' (Tickell, 2011, p58). While continuing to recognise observational assessment as fundamental to curriculum planning, Tickell recommended that practitioners be clear that recording assessments was different to actually making assessments and not all assessments need to be recorded in writing. She clarified that assessment is an on-going process that informs how practitioners respond to children, through planning learning experiences to ensure they make progress.

An important addition to the revised EYFS that also impacted assessment and planning was the introduction of the Characteristics of Effective Learning and Teaching (DfE, 2012). This was significant because it highlighted the purpose and importance of planning, not only for academic outcomes, but also for children's dispositions to learning. This shifted the focus to include planning for *how* children learn as well as *what* children learn. A third significant amendment that impacted assessment and planning was the changes made to the areas of learning and development. Tickell recommended that there be seven areas of learning and development instead of six. Taking account of extensive research that was emerging about language and communication and its impact on lifelong learning, Tickell recommended that communication and language be taken out of the area of literacy and included as an area of learning in its own right. To further emphasise its importance, this area was positioned as a prime area of learning and development alongside physical development and personal, social and emotional development. The remaining four areas were labelled as specific areas of learning and development and these were: Literacy, Mathematics, Understanding the World and Expressive Arts and Design. The revised EYFS became statutory in September 2012 and its accompanying guidance, *Development Matters in the Early Years Foundation Stage* (Early Education, 2012) was also revised to reflect the new 2012 version of the EYFS. Since then, there have only been minor revisions to the EYFS framework in 2014 and 2017, in order to update some of the legislation within the safeguarding and welfare requirements. It is the current *EYFS Statutory Framework* (DfE, 2017) and its accompanying guidance, *Development Matters* (Early Education, 2012) that will be discussed in the following section.

THE CURRENT EARLY YEARS FOUNDATION STAGE

Two main documents that support providers and practitioners to implement the Early Years Foundation Stage are:

- *The Statutory Framework for the Early Years Foundation Stage* (DfE, 2017); and
- *Development Matters in the Early Years Foundation Stage* (Early Education, 2012).

THE *STATUTORY FRAMEWORK FOR THE EARLY YEARS FOUNDATION STAGE*

The *Statutory Framework for the Early Years Foundation Stage* (DfE, 2017) is the document that is legally binding for all Ofsted registered Early Years providers. It outlines the legal requirements for learning and development, assessment and the safeguarding and welfare of children. It promotes a principled, play-based pedagogy and lists the Early Learning Goals that are the expected outcomes for children at the end of the Reception year, which is the end point of the EYFS. This document is the one that registered providers use to ensure that they are fulfilling all the legal requirements for running an EYFS setting or an EYFS class in a school. Practitioners also refer to this document to ensure that their practice is meeting the statutory requirements, but for more detailed guidance on how to support young children's learning and development, most practitioners use *Development Matters in the Early Years Foundation Stage* (Early Education, 2012) in their daily practice.

DEVELOPMENT MATTERS IN THE EARLY YEARS FOUNDATION STAGE

It is vitally important to recognise that *Development Matters in the Early Years Foundation Stage* (Early Education, 2012) is not an EYFS curriculum or a planning tool. The opening statement from *Development Matters* makes it clear that it is a guidance document to support understanding of how young children learn and develop.

> *This guidance helps adults to understand and support each individual child's development pathway. Other guidance is provided at www.foundationyears.org.uk.*

(Early Education, 2012, p1)

Development Matters (Early Education, 2012) is intended to be used alongside other resources to support your assessment of children's learning and development and it is the assessment of what children know and can do and how they learn that will inform your planning. There are development charts provided for each of the seven areas of learning and development and each one is divided into six age phases in months, which overlap with each other (see Early Education, 2012 for these charts). By overlapping the age brackets in the development charts, the authors intended to give the message that learning and development are not necessarily linear. Piaget's maturation theory (Piaget, 2001) proposed a linear approach to learning and development. Socio-cultural theorists such as Vygotsky (1896–1924) and Bronfenbrenner (1917–2005), however, expanded this theory, highlighting the important influence of the child's culture and upbringing on their learning and development (Neaum, 2013). Thus, for some children a linear progression through the milestones in *Development Matters* may be the norm, but for others their journey may move in non-linear directions, progressing through some of the development milestones and missing others and often occasionally moving sideways across different areas of learning and development. The learning and development grids that accompany each area of learning are not intended to be used as checklists or as learning objectives for planning purposes. The guidance clearly stipulates that:

> *Children develop at their own rates, and in their own ways. The development statements and their order should not be taken as necessary steps for individual children. They should not be used as checklists.*

(Early Education, 2012, p6)

Thus, for planning purposes you will need a sound knowledge and understanding of child development theory. *Development Matters* is very useful in guiding you through typical patterns of development but it only provides a snapshot of the many milestones that children may reach along their development journey towards the Early Learning Goals. More detailed child development textbooks will support you to carry out more authentic assessments of children and plan more appropriately for their next steps.

REFLECTION ACTIVITY 1.1

How does your setting use *Development Matters in the Early Years Foundation Stage*?

Why should the development statements in *Development Matters* not be used as checklists?

What is your opinion on this?

USING *DEVELOPMENT MATTERS* TO SUPPORT ASSESSMENT AND PLANNING

As you read through this chapter, refer to the first five pages of *Development Matters in the Early Years Foundation Stage* (Early Education, 2012). The information on these pages reflects a child-centred pedagogical approach to assessment and planning in the EYFS. On page 2 of *Development Matters*, the four principles that underpin the EYFS framework are described and there are examples provided of how to apply them in practice. On page 3, the cycle of observation, assessment and planning is shown in a diagram that links the cycle to the four principles of the EYFS. The first of these principles, the Unique Child, is the starting place for planning. This is the point where the practitioner observes the child and assesses what they know and can do, as well as how they learn. The second and third principles, Positive Relationships and Enabling Environments, are where the practitioner begins to plan what they can do to promote learning (how they interact with the children) and what they can provide (how they resource the learning environment). Together, these principles, within the cycle of observation, assessment and planning, should lead to successful learning and development.

On page 4 of *Development Matters*, the guidance reminds us that *how* children learn (Characteristics of Effective Learning) and *what* children learn (areas of learning and development) are interconnected. The EYFS is all about laying firm foundations for learning so that children have potential to become independent, lifelong learners. Therefore, this is the key stage in which acute attention needs to be given to supporting the development of strong dispositions to learning, which are described in the EYFS as the 'Characteristics of Effective Learning'. There are two useful charts on page 5 of *Development Matters*, which provide a quick reference overview of the Characteristics of Effective Learning alongside the seven areas of learning and development. Each area of learning and development is divided into two or more aspects (e.g. Literacy is made up of two aspects, which are reading and writing). For each aspect of learning there is an Early Learning Goal, which is the age-related expectation for children at the end of the EYFS; the end of the Reception year in school.

The areas of learning and development and the many aspects that are covered within them, together with the Characteristics of Effective Learning are all interconnected (see page 4). Therefore, planning for the EYFS needs to be holistic, flexible and personalised as much as is possible, so that all children are supported to make progress.

USING THE PRINCIPLES OF THE EYFS IN PLANNING FOR LEARNING

The four principles outlined on page 2 of the guidance have implications for practitioners when planning for learning. The Unique Child is the starting point for child-centred planning. This principle recognises the individuality of each child and reminds us that children are constantly learning through every interaction and experience they have. It respects the capability of children and states that they can be 'resilient, capable, confident and self-assured' (Early Education, 2012, p2). The implications of this, when planning for learning, are that you are required to get to know your key children or your class really well. Through observing them and interacting with them you will more easily be able to tune in to their interests and notice their capabilities. Then, you will be able to respond to what their interests and learning needs are. Putting this principle of the Unique Child into practice involves observation and assessment, which is the start of the planning process. However, this is dependent on having a good knowledge and understanding of child development. You need to be able to assess whether the child is displaying typical learning and development for their chronological age, so that support and interventions can be put in place to ensure that each child makes progress. The development descriptors in *Development Matters* are not sufficient on their own to enable you to make a secure judgement about this. Therefore, for planning purposes you should continually update and refresh your knowledge of child development.

The second principle, Positive Relationships, is based on Bowlby's attachment theory (Bowlby, 1953). It recognises the importance of a secure and loving relationship for children to be able to develop and become independent. When planning for learning, this principle urges you to reflect on how you respond to children. Positive relationships are formed through your interactions and emotional connection with children. This can be challenging at times, especially if you are balancing many priorities or during a busy time. It requires you to plan in advance and to plan in the moment, thinking about your choice of questions, vocabulary, actions and style of communication. Positive relationships are enacted through everything that you do and young children are very perceptive in noticing and being influenced by what you do. Therefore, when planning in the EYFS, you should consider carefully your role as a key person or as the significant adult in the setting. Whether you are planning in advance or responding in the moment, you should reflect on how your relationships with children foster in them a sense of importance and belonging.

The third principle, Enabling Environments, is concerned with creating an ethos and a physical space in which people and learning are valued. This principle relates to what you provide for children. The environment is seen as both physical and emotional. The implications of this for planning purposes require you to choose physical resources matched to children's ages and stages of development and to be able to present them in ways that enthuse and motivate children to become involved. This requires you to have a good knowledge of child development and an enthusiastic and positive attitude to learning. Planning for the emotional environment may require a more subtle approach, but it is of equal importance to the physical environment. It involves thoughtful planning for care routines, transitions, staffing, ratios, key person times and many other hidden aspects of your curriculum.

The final principle, Learning and Development, emphasises the need for a child-centred approach to planning. It confirms that all children are different and all children are unique. They learn and develop in different ways, and therefore they require you to know them individually and respond in different ways that support their unique development pathways. Putting this principle into practice in the context of planning in the EYFS involves being tuned in to the learning needs of your children and planning playful and challenging opportunities for them to develop across all areas of learning. This may be through planning in advance for learning through activities and experiences matched to their stage of development or it may involve capitalising on learning opportunities as they arise and providing extra challenges through your interactions and responses to them in the moment when they are learning.

Taken as a whole, these four principles are threaded through *Development Matters* in a way that supports assessment and planning. Each page denoting the Characteristics of Effective Learning (pages 6–7) and the development grids for the areas of learning and development (pages 9–46) contains three columns for each of the first three principles of the EYFS. This is useful for supporting assessment and planning. Each column labelled 'Unique Child' lists descriptors of what children can do. These are descriptions of typical learning behaviours or development milestones. These are not learning objectives but more similar to learning outcomes, in the sense that they describe the knowledge and skills that children may acquire. These may be used as a support for making assessment judgements and are useful for spotting when a child may be displaying atypical development, that which is outside of the expected parameters for their age range. These milestones are not to be used as checklists. The column headed Positive Relationships sets out suggestions for how adults may respond to children at different stages of development. The statements in these columns outline what you could do next to support progress. The column headed Enabling Environments sets out suggestions for what you could provide to enable children to make progress.

FACTORS THAT INFLUENCE HOW YOU PLAN FOR LEARNING

As previously stated, there is no prescriptive way for planning that will work for everyone. This is because planning for learning in the EYFS is personalised to individuals, groups and cohorts of children. The EYFS is a diverse sector covering a wide age range (0–5 years) in a wide variety of different settings. A childminder's planning for children at home will be vastly different to a Reception class teacher's planning for 30 children in a classroom. This is why you must use your knowledge of child development and your knowledge of your children to make professional decisions about how to plan effectively for learning, based on the EYFS statutory requirements. There are many examples of commercially produced planning pro-formas available via the internet. Although these are useful for practitioners to consider how other settings are recording their planning, they will need to be adapted and tailored to meet the needs of your children and the requirements of your setting. There are some examples of planning presented within this book, but they are not intended to be replicated by other settings. Rather, they are presented as case study examples for you to reflect upon and make professionally informed decisions about how to record your planning within the cycle of observation, assessment and planning in your unique situation. You will need to take into account many different factors that will influence how you are able to plan for learning. Some key questions to consider when starting out are:

- What is the purpose of planning?
- Who is the planning for?
- What needs to be included in the planning for the children in my setting?

REFLECTION ACTIVITY 1.2

Make a list of reasons why we should plan for learning in the EYFS.

Use your answers to help you reflect on the following questions:

- Who needs to see your planning?
- Who uses it?
- Does all planning need to be written down?

EYFS STATUTORY REQUIREMENTS FOR PLANNING

Although there appears to be only minimum guidance in the *EYFS Statutory Framework* (DfE, 2017) on how to plan for learning, the requirements make it clear that:

> *Practitioners must consider the individual needs, interests, and stage of development of each child in their care, and must use this information to plan a challenging and enjoyable experience for each child in all of the areas of learning and development.*

> (DfE, 2017, p9)

What is striking in this requirement is that planning must take account of each individual child. Therefore, it is crucial that you plan time to observe children and also spend time with them, interacting and getting to know each one as an individual. It is also significant that the experiences you plan for children must be 'challenging and enjoyable' in relation to 'all areas of learning and development'. All children are different and therefore, the levels of challenge will also reflect this. Planning for groups will need to be differentiated and when planning for any area of learning and development, you will need to consider whether the experience is indeed challenging and enjoyable. This requires a creative and holistic approach to all areas of learning so that the areas are not planned for in isolation, but overlap and interconnect. The *EYFS Statutory Framework* offers guidance on how the areas of learning and development relate to each other and how to plan appropriately for the different age phases with the EYFS:

> *Practitioners working with the youngest children are expected to focus strongly on the three prime areas, which are the basis for successful learning in the other four specific areas.*

> (DfE, 2017, p9)

It is important to note the word 'strongly' and not mistake it as meaning 'exclusively'. The EYFS guidance gives a clear message that all areas of learning are interconnected and interdependent. Babies and toddlers learn through all seven areas of learning and development, even though strong attention must be given to the prime areas to ensure that these are fully embedded. As stated in the *Statutory Framework*,

> *It is expected that the balance will shift towards a more equal focus on all areas of learning as children grow in confidence and ability within the three prime areas.*

> (DfE, 2017, p9)

PLANNING THROUGH PLAY

The *EYFS Statutory Framework* (DfE, 2017) is informed by theory of how children learn and develop. It promotes a child-centred, play-based pedagogy in relation to planning:

> *Each area of learning and development must be implemented through planned, purposeful play and through a mix of adult-led and child-initiated activity. Play is essential for children's development, building their confidence as they learn to explore, to think about problems, and relate to others.*

> (DfE, 2017, p9)

Planning for play requires you to plan a high quality learning environment in which children can make choices, experiment, make connections, take risks and independently interact with open-ended resources that support all areas of learning and development. For this purpose, most settings would have in place a long-term plan for 'continuous provision'. Continuous provision refers to how the physical environment is divided into discrete areas of provision with resources that are permanently available for children to explore and return to for child-initiated learning. For example, a sensory area, a creative area, a block play area, a role play area are just some of the different continuous provision areas that may be offered in an EYFS setting. However, continuous provision also includes the care and learning routines that provide a predictable and stable pattern to the day, and opportunities for parents and carers to be involved and contribute to their children's learning. Planning for these experiences should take into account the diverse needs of the children and families in your particular setting.

✓ TIPS FOR PRACTICE

Planning for continuous provision must also include the outdoor area. Look for opportunities to include greater physical challenges in the outdoor area and let the children experience all weather types. Children and practitioners will be willing to play outside if they have suitable clothing.

When planning for learning through play the EYFS stipulates that practitioners must include opportunities for children to learn, 'by leading their own play, and by taking part in play which is guided by adults' (DfE, 2017, p9). Therefore, within the planning there needs to be a balance between child led activities and adult led activities and the EYFS reminds us that:

> *There is an ongoing judgement to be made by practitioners about the balance between activities led by children, and activities led or guided by adults. Practitioners must respond to each child's emerging needs and interests, guiding their development through warm, positive interaction. As children grow older, and as their development allows, it is expected that the balance will gradually shift towards more activities led by adults, to help children prepare for more formal learning, ready for Year 1.*

> (DfE, 2017, p9)

Therefore, it is expected that planning for babies and toddlers will be plans for individuals including planning for care routines, with a gradual shift towards group and cohort planning for Pre-school or Nursery class children. Then, when children enter the Reception class, more emphasis will likely be given to whole class weekly planning for literacy, mathematics, phonics and continuous provision. However, it is important to note that all children are unique and there is never an age phase in which individual planning is not appropriate. The key to effective planning is to reflect upon and respond to children's individual needs and interests.

BRINGING IT ALL TOGETHER

The *EYFS Statutory Framework* (DfE, 2017) provides statutory requirements for practitioners to adhere to when planning for learning. These requirements promote the importance of planning for individual needs, learning through play and taking account of how children learn. Most settings bring these requirements together by planning for some or all of the following aspects of provision: ·

1. Long-term planning – depending on the age group of the children, this may include any of the following:

    •   planning for the physical learning environment (areas of continuous provision);
    •   planning for care routines;
    •   planning for the daily routine to meet the setting's requirements (e.g. meal times, assemblies in school);
    •   planning for predictable festivals and seasons throughout the year.

2. Medium-term planning – not all settings use medium-term planning, but for older children and particularly in schools, it is common to plan for learning across a number of weeks. This may be in response to external factors such as the setting having a shared space for two classes, sharing resources or needing to adhere to curriculum planning policies. For most settings medium-term planning involves planning for progress over time through a topic of interest. Usually, this will also include planning enhancements to the areas of continuous provision (e.g. enhancing the role-play area to support learning through the current topic).

3. Short-term planning – depending on the age group of the children this may involve weekly or daily plans to address individual and group learning needs. Daily plans may include planning in advance what you intend to provide for children and how you intend to respond to them, but daily planning may also be 'in the moment', i.e. how you respond to a child or children's play through your choices of interaction and the resources you provide at the point when learning is taking place. These types of plans are recorded in various ways, for example, through annotations on weekly plans.

CONCLUSION

This chapter has provided you with an overview of the background and context in which you will be planning for children's learning in the EYFS. It has highlighted the importance of child-centred planning and supported you to meet the requirements for planning outlined in the *EYFS Statutory Framework*. It has set out guidance on how to use the non-statutory guidance *Development Matters* to inform the decisions you make when planning for individual needs. Specifically, it has highlighted the need for you to utilise your observation and assessment skills and your knowledge of child development when you are planning for learning in the EYFS. The chapter also acknowledges that there are many external factors which influence your planning and your preferred pedagogical approach. Most importantly, it suggests that the learning needs of the individual children you care for must be at the heart of your decision-making when you plan all aspects of your provision.

FURTHER READING

McEvoy, J (2018) Early Years Curriculum, in McMahon, S and Dyer, M (eds) *Work Based Practice in the Early Years*. Abingdon: Routledge, pp53–68.
Palaiologou, I (2013) *The Early Years Foundation Stage: Theory and Practice* (2nd edn). London: Sage.

REFERENCES

Bowlby, J (1953) *Child Care and the Growth of Love*. London: Penguin Books.
Department for Children, Schools and Families (DCSF) (2008) *Statutory Framework for the Early Years Foundation Stage*. Nottingham: DCSF.
Department for Education (2012) *The Statutory Framework for the Early Years Foundation Stage*. London: DfE.
Department for Education (2014) *The Statutory Framework for the Early Years Foundation Stage*. London: DfE.
Department for Education (2017) *Statutory Framework for the Early Years Foundation Stage: Setting the Standards for Learning, Development and Care for Children from Birth to Five*. London: DfE.
Department for Education and Skills (DfES) (2004) *Every Child Matters, Change for Children*. London: HMSO.
Early Education (2012) *Development Matters in the Early Years Foundation Stage (EYFS)*. London: Early Education. Available at https://www.foundationyears.org.uk/wp-content/uploads/2012/03/Development-Matters-FINAL-PRINT-AMENDED.pdf
Neaum, S (2013) *Child Development for Early Years Students and Practitioners* (2nd edn). London: Sage.
Piaget, J (2001) *The Psychology of Intelligence*. London: Routledge.
Tickell, C (2011) *The Early Years: Foundations for Life, Health and Learning*. London: Department for Education.

2 PRINCIPLES OF PLANNING

Amanda Crow and Nicola Firth

CHAPTER AIMS

By the end of this chapter you will be able to:

- understand the principles for planning in the Early Years Foundation Stage, including the Characteristics of Effective Learning (CoEL)
- understand key points of theory underpinning planning
- understand how effective observation and assessment are the basis of planning for children
- make use of various approaches to planning, including holistic, inclusive, flexible and collaborative, to meet individual children's needs

As you read this chapter, refer to pages 5–7 of *Development Matters in the Early Years Foundation Stage (EYFS)* (Early Education, 2012).

INTRODUCTION

In this chapter you will learn about how observation and assessment inform the principles of effective planning for children. Topics will include planning that incorporates:

- Characteristics of Effective Learning (Early Education, 2012, p4);
- collaborative, holistic and inclusive approaches to planning including children, parents, practitioners and agencies who may be involved with the child and their family;
- planning for children's individual care, learning and development needs.

If these principles are taken into account, the child's 'next steps' will be planned for effectively. Practitioners may use the *Early Years Foundation Stage Development Matters* guidance (Early Education, 2012), to assess and plan for children's needs. The Early Years Foundation Stage Statutory Framework (EYFS) states that 'early years providers must guide the development of children's capabilities' (DfE, 2017, p7) and the way in which practitioners can do this effectively is through observing, assessing and planning carefully and thoroughly. Throughout the chapter we will relate to 'children', which includes babies, toddlers and children to the age of 5, who are all learning and developing in the Early Years Foundation Stage.

It is imperative when planning for children to consider planning for both care needs and learning and development. The *Development Matters* guidance advises practitioners to 'use the development statements to identify possible areas in which to challenge and extend the child's current learning and development' (Early Education, 2012, p3). In order to be able to do this and plan for care, learning and development needs, it is essential to follow the 'observe, assess and plan' cycle, as shown in Figure 2.1.

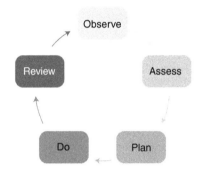

Figure 2.1   The planning cycle (adapted from Early Education, 2012)

Without observing a child in the first instance you cannot assess their care needs or developmental milestones; therefore, planning for the child would be unsuccessful. Within the cycle the child is central and the most important person. The cycle works in this way:

1. **'Observe'** the child regularly and note what you see;
2. **'Assess'** the child's care needs and learning and development using *Development Matters* (Early Education, 2012), and record your judgements;
3. **'Plan'** for the child's next steps in order to enhance their learning and development;
4. **'Do'** what has been planned for the child, but do take into account this must be flexible and adapted accordingly; 'reflect-in-action' (Schön, 1991);
5. **'Review'** the planned care, learning and development needs and/or activities and start the cycle again.

Using this approach adopts a continuous planning cycle for children, as practitioners will plan for individuals and groups, including activity plans, trips to places of interest, planning for continuous provision and enhancing areas of provision.

PLANNING FOR CHARACTERISTICS OF EFFECTIVE LEARNING

Children are born ready, able and eager to learn (Early Education, 2012). This is a profound statement that underpins the philosophy of the Early Years Foundation Stage Framework and informs *Development Matters*, the supporting non-statutory guidance. Adults, parents/carers and practitioners who care for children, therefore, are in a privileged position as they have the responsibility to ensure children have the right opportunities to grow, develop and learn from their early experiences and the environments they encounter.

Each child is unique, developing at their own individual pace and as such it is important that parents and practitioners work together to support their early development. *Development Matters* introduces us to the ways children interconnect with people and their environment through the Characteristics of Effective Learning (CoEL) (Early Education, 2012: 4). This enables the child to be regarded as a unique individual who is able to learn through playing and exploring their home, Nursery setting and the wider environment.

There are a number of child development theories that underpin the CoEL, in particular the human ecological model proposed by Uri Bronfenbrenner. The model focuses on the importance of the environment, people and the many influences that affect children's lives. Bronfenbrenner's theory (1979) proposes that children's development is influenced by different levels or strata in society. Simply put, these levels can be described as different layers that contain people and resources in society that influence the way children are brought up.

Bronfenbrenner's theory is often represented as a network of concentric circles – circles that have a common centre (see Figure 2.2). The common centre, for Bronfenbrenner, is the child, who is then surrounded by their immediate and extended family, friends and the wider community including Nursery and schools, referred to as a microsystem. What is also significant is the way children's lives are influenced by relationships in the wider cultural and political world. Children are affected by the beliefs, attitudes and behaviours of the wider community, local authorities and the government, and the policies and laws they implement (Jackson and Needham, 2014).

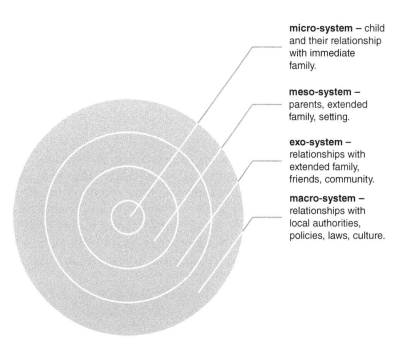

micro-system – child and their relationship with immediate family.

meso-system – parents, extended family, setting.

exo-system – relationships with extended family, friends, community.

macro-system – relationships with local authorities, policies, laws, culture.

Figure 2.2 Ecological systems model (adapted from Bronfenbrenner, 1979)

Parallels can be seen between Bronfenbrenner's ecological model and the CoEL; for example, the unique child at the centre developing in the context of their individual families and cultures. We understand that children learn best when they have positive relationships and that they develop well when they are safe, secure and have a sense of belonging (Early Education, 2012, p2). You can use the model in Figure 2.2 to support your planning as this will guide and help you to recognise the needs of the unique child, ensuring you do not plan in isolation, but take into account the many different relationships and influences they encounter.

REFLECTION ACTIVITY 2.1

Think about a child that you know, ideally a child you care for in your practice:

- using Bronfenbrenner's model, draw a set of concentric circles and place the child's name at the centre;
- now add all the different influences, people and services that may have an impact on their lives.

Recreating Bronfenbrenner's model for a child at your setting will help you to understand the different people and services you may need to consider when planning for the child's individual needs, for example:

1. Who do they live with, how many siblings and what about their extended family?
2. How many hours do they attend the setting, do they have other people who care for them outside the setting – grandparents, or other forms of childcare for example?
3. Do they have any extended services involved in their lives, perhaps a health visitor, speech therapist or occupational health practitioner?

When you have completed your own ecological model, can you see how important it is for you to consider the ways children engage with other people and their environment? Using theoretical models such as this helps you to understand the importance of using theory to support your practice and this in turn helps you to be confident as a practitioner.

The CoEL are characterised by three main principles: playing and exploring, active learning, and creating and thinking critically (Early Education, 2012, p4). Children learn through being active and from watching and imitating others – the principles of CoEL, together with the prime and specific areas, enable children to learn and develop at their own pace and are fundamental for children to reach their full potential. When planning learning experiences for children, practitioners should take account of both *prime* and *specific* areas of learning in order to ensure they meet the needs of the individual children in their care.

Development Matters describes the prime areas as the areas of development that emerge early in response to the different relationships and experiences a child encounters (Table 2.1). They are fundamental and work together (Early Education, 2012). Simply put, they are the foundation on which all learning develops. The prime areas are:

- personal, social and emotional development;
- communication and language;
- physical development.

Table 2.1 CoEL and the areas of learning and development

Characteristics of Effective Learning	Area of Learning and Development	Aspect
Playing and exploring – engagement	**Prime Areas**	
Finding out and exploring	**Personal, Social and Emotional Development**	Making relationships
		Self-confidence and self-awareness
Playing with what they know		Managing feelings and behaviour
Being willing to 'have a go'	**Physical Development**	Moving and handling
		Health and self-care
Active learning – motivation	**Communication and Language**	Listening and attention
		Understanding
Being involved and concentrating		Speaking
Keeping trying	**Specific areas**	
	Literacy	Reading
Enjoying achieving what they set out to do		Writing
	Mathematics	Numbers
Creating and thinking critically – thinking		Shape, space and measure
	Understanding the World	People and communities
Having their own ideas		The world
Making links		Technology
	Expressive Arts and Design	Exploring and using media and materials
Choosing ways to do things		Being imaginative

Reproduced from Early Education, 2012.

PLANNING FOR AND ENHANCING AREAS OF PROVISION

To ensure the CoEL principles, playing and exploring, active learning, and creating and thinking critically (Early Education, 2012, p4) are considered throughout the setting, practitioners must think about planning appropriate continuous provision. Continuous provision develops long-term planning and relates to resources that are available and continually accessible for children at all times that will enhance their learning and development. Open-ended resources will be available that encourage children to explore and investigate throughout their free-flow play and these will be linked to the children's interests through the use of the observation cycle (see Figure 2.1). Continuous provision supports the 'enabling environment' of the setting which is integral to the overarching principles of the Early Years Foundation Stage Statutory Framework (EYFS) (DfE, 2017). It is recognised in the EYFS that children learn and develop in 'enabling environments'; however, they all 'develop and learn in different ways' (DfE, 2017, p6) and this needs to be taken into account when planning for continuous provision. Continuous provision resources will be changed throughout the year as children develop and learn.

✓ **TIPS FOR PRACTICE**

To ensure that continuous provision supports the changing needs of children it is important to regularly check, or audit, the resources available in each area. For example, in the painting area children aged 24 months will typically paint at an easel on a large piece of paper with a large brush, using two or three ready mixed colours in non-spill pots. They may also want to explore the paint with their fingers and mouths. A child of 48 months should have access to a range of different paints with opportunities to mix colours and media. You might want to introduce them to new techniques and the work of artists. They need to be able to choose from a range of paint brushes and tools which reflect their developing fine motor skills, present suitable challenges and allow them to refine their work.

PLANNING IN PARTNERSHIP

The EYFS (2017, p6) states 'children learn and develop well in enabling environments, in which their experiences respond to their individual needs and there is a strong partnership between practitioners and parents and/or carers'. Developing relationships and planning for children's care, learning and development needs are integral to the principles of planning. Collaborative working between practitioners and parents can enhance the planning process and ensure children's learning and development is supported between the home and Early Years setting. It is recognised as good practice that quality partnerships between practitioners and parents leads to effective relationships, resulting in positive learning experiences between the home and Early Years setting (Mukherji and Dryden, 2014). Case study 2.1 shows how a private day Nursery works in collaboration with a parent to plan for her daughter's care, learning and development needs.

CASE STUDY 2.1

Before starting Nursery

Kate has a 26-month-old daughter, Lauren, who has attended a private day Nursery from 13 months old. Prior to starting Nursery, Kate stayed at home on maternity leave. Kate and Lauren's father decided to place her in a private day Nursery upon returning to work three days per week. Lauren visited the Nursery on various occasions for one month prior to starting and these visits were planned between Kate and the Nursery, starting with short visits with Kate staying with Lauren and leading to longer lengths of time with Kate leaving Lauren to settle with the practitioners. The Nursery manager and Lauren's pre-allocated key person also did a home visit and asked Kate various questions about Lauren – for example, individual care and development needs, likes and dislikes and routine at home; these all assisted the key person in planning appropriately for

Lauren's care, learning and development. The Nursery tries to mirror the baby's routines at home and Kate said they did this well, but there was some variation in terms of meal times due to the Nursery routine.

Key person and transitions to new rooms

Lauren settled into Nursery in the baby room and remained under the supervision of her pre-allocated key person. When Lauren started Nursery she preferred relationships with one person, rather than multiple relationships. Lauren, however, developed a stronger bond with another practitioner in the baby room, but remained with the pre-allocated key person. Upon moving to the under 2s room, which Kate says was a smooth transition, Lauren was allocated a new key person, but again developed a stronger bond with another practitioner but again remained with the pre-allocated key person. Kate doesn't think this caused a problem, as all the practitioners cared for, observed and planned for all the babies. Lauren has recently moved to the under 3s room; however, this transition did not go as smoothly. Kate was informed that Lauren would be starting visits to prepare for the move; however, Kate was not told when or how they would be planned. Kate did not know Lauren had started the visits until she had done her second visit and was told when she collected her at the end of the day. Kate had not been offered an opportunity to look around Lauren's new room or to meet any of the practitioners. Nevertheless, the practitioner who Lauren had formed a strong bond with tended to go on the visits with Lauren and is now based in the room as Lauren's key person. Kate is pleased with this, as she feels Lauren has a strong relationship with this particular practitioner who plans effectively for Lauren, making the connections between the home and Nursery environment.

How the practitioners plan in partnership with parents

The Nursery uses an electronic communications app linked to parents' phones. The app includes observations, photographs and videos, the child's next steps and links to *Development Matters* milestones, and all of these are shared with parents throughout the child's day. Kate receives various observations of Lauren during the day and can comment on these. An example is a video of Lauren singing 'The Wheels on the Bus' with the practitioner making links to milestones and planning for Lauren's next steps. Kate commented on this, stating that Lauren sings 'Twinkle Twinkle Little Star' at home, and was able to send the comment directly to the app for the practitioner to read. Kate thinks this is extremely useful in planning for Lauren's learning and development and making the links between the home and Nursery environment, including keeping Kate informed about Lauren's development.

Kate's closing comments

> I think the Nursery are very good at keeping up with development stages and were excellent and supportive when Lauren was very poorly. They gave one-to-one care, medication, changed days and even gave a small refund for unattended days. In terms of development, I would just like there to be a bit more involvement with more structure to conversations, rather than just at pick-up and drop-off time, for example formal meetings.

Kate did, however, say parents can request meetings, but it would make her feel better if the Nursery planned these; as she said, she doesn't want to be seen as the '*paranoid parent*' always asking questions.

A successful partnership develops through trusting relationships. This takes time and investment from all parties and does not happen overnight. Parents can sometimes feel that professionals 'know best' due to their knowledge of child development and Early Years practice. This is somewhat evident in the case study at the end of Kate's closing comments, when she talks about being seen as a 'paranoid parent', as Kate is assuming that the practitioners will label her if she asks too many questions. Arnold (2017) suggests that practitioners should be aware of this potential power imbalance when developing relationships and sharing what has happened in a 'child's day'. Investing time early in the relationship to find out about daily routines and the important people in the child's life will help the partnership start from a point of equal respect. Many settings start this process by conducting a home visit, usually by the 'key person', and this can be an opportune time to build the foundations for a strong and trusting partnership. This also provides an opportunity for the parents/carers and practitioners to plan transitions together. This type of approach is clearly evident in the case study with Kate and the practitioners planning a smooth transition from Lauren's home environment to the Nursery environment. Kate does feel that there are trusting relationships between herself and the practitioners, and this was the case from before Lauren started Nursery permanently.

✓ TIPS FOR PRACTICE

Accommodate children bringing in a 'transition' object from home. This might be a soft toy, blanket or a toy train. This helps them to maintain a connection with home and feel secure. Ensure parents get the opportunity to visit each room before a transition so they can become familiar with the routine and the staff.

Planning for transition to Nursery enables all the key adults to acknowledge any worries, share the children's likes and dislikes and any other important information. It also provides the practitioner with key information about the child in their home environment. It is helpful to refer back to Bronfenbrenner at this point and the way that different relationships may affect transition. Considering how children may be supported effectively by their key adults will help children to settle and accept their changing environment. Crow and Froggett (2017) identify that the key person system results in developing relationships with parents and that this will continue to develop over time. Referring back to the case study, when Lauren started Nursery and made the transition to the under 2s room she was pre-allocated key persons; however, she formed a stronger bond with two other practitioners.

REFLECTION ACTIVITY 2.2

Should the practitioners with whom Lauren formed a stronger bond have become her key person, in order to ensure that planning was effective in meeting her care, learning and development needs?

Upon moving to the under 3s room, the transition seemingly was not as well planned; however, the practitioner with whom Lauren formed a strong bond in the under 2s room moved with her and became her key person. Therefore, you can see good practice with this approach, which is supported in the trusting relationship between Kate and Lauren's key person.

PLANNING THROUGH CHILDREN'S INTERESTS AND INDIVIDUAL NEEDS

In order to plan for children's interests, you will need to regularly observe them to see what they are doing and talking about. Keyte-Hartland (2018, p10) suggests that the practitioner must 'see the ideas and thinking that is going on beneath' the child's actions. Therefore, it is not only what you see, but also what you hear and how you interpret their actions. It is essential that you continually observe for children's interests to ensure they are engaged in their learning and development. The CoEL state that if children have well-planned opportunities to play and explore, then this will encourage engagement in their learning and development (Early Education, 2012). You can ensure this happens through making sure their interests are brought into your planning for individual children and groups, as groups of children will often have the same types of interests. It is also essential that you talk to parents regularly about their child's interests in the home environment, so you can make the all-important links between what they like to do at home and the implementation of activities and opportunities in the setting.

REFLECTION ACTIVITY 2.3

Consider yourself as key person for Lauren from the case study in the 'Planning in partnership' section of the chapter. You are planning for Lauren and need to ensure her interests are further developed through activities, interactions and resources. Answer the following questions:

1. Parents can lead very busy lives and you will also be busy in your job roles. Often, drop-off and collection is one of the busiest times in a setting. How will you plan to meet regularly with Lauren's parents, so you can make links between her interests in the home environment and the activities she undertakes in the setting?
2. You will not only have Lauren's individual interests to plan for, but also a number of other children. How will you ensure that Lauren's interests are planned for and documented?

Every child's individual needs must be met and this is done through not only planning for their interests, but ensuring their individual care needs are met. If you are working with babies you will find yourself planning for individual care needs much more than a child who is developing their own self-care needs; for example, a 3-year-old who can go to the toilet independently. Babies should have care plans, which will include feeding times, sleep routines, nappy changing etc. and the plan must attempt to mirror the home routine. It is usually the key person's responsibility to keep the plans up-to-date, as these will change regularly, as the babies' needs change. It is vital that you maintain regular discussions and meetings with parents, so care plans are regularly updated. This may also be the case with children who have particular special educational needs and disabilities (SEND), as they may have very specific care needs. Therefore, do not only think about babies in the context of care plans, but also about children who have a SEND. It is important to remember that babies and children all develop at different rates, so no two care plans will look the same.

HOLISTIC PLANNING AND INCLUSIVE PRACTICE

Children's development is not something a practitioner can predict; each child is unique and, therefore, their development will not follow a predicted path. The term or concept of taking a 'child-centred' approach is often used by practitioners to describe the way they tune into children's individual needs. Taking a holistic or all-inclusive approach when developing planning in the Early Years setting enables the practitioner to reflect on the many different ways children explore their worlds. This approach to practice is supported in the EYFS and through the CoEL, through the prime and specific areas (DfE, 2017, p10).

Holistic planning recognises the importance of understanding the child and how their diverse experiences shape and impact on their development. It makes a connection between the physical, cognitive and psychological well-being of children, and particularly how practitioners see the ways in which the child's development and learning are interconnected. Supporting the principle of the 'unique child' in practice means that practitioners value and respect children's experiences, their similarities and differences, and identify any need for individual support (Early Education, 2012). Consequently, holistic planning is an approach that is inclusive; Hallet (2016) explains this principle well by describing the importance of seeing the child as one who has individual strengths and attributes. Inclusive practice ensures all children have equality of opportunity, that they are valued for who they are and are provided with an environment that promotes their health, education and well-being.

Engaging in practice that enables you to tune in to and identify children's interests will help you to plan holistically. This does mean that you might need to challenge your own and other's practice. Holistic planning means that children are enabled to explore their own interests and that knowledgeable practitioners support them to do so. Holistic planning does not, therefore, mean that all children should engage in the same activity at the same time, or reach the same developmental milestone at the same age. Every child is unique in their own way and will develop physical, intellectual, language, emotional and social development in their own time. There will be times, however, when concerns are raised regarding specific areas of development if a child starts to show signs that development is not progressing as it should, and the holistic planning approach will support signs of any additional support needs they may have.

Child development theorist Piaget considered the child to be a 'lone scientist' where they explore their world and start to make sense of how the world works around them, and the 'people, objects and events within it' (Dyer, 2017, p75). Therefore, you must plan for their learning with this in mind and try to take yourself to the level of the child and their way of thinking and categorising and working out how the world works. According to Piaget, children between the ages of 18 months to 6 years are in the pre-operational stage where they base reasoning on their own experiences and perceptions and not those of others around them (Garhart Mooney, 2000), so when planning it is important to remember this and plan around the interests and activities they enjoy.

REFLECTION ACTIVITY 2.4

Consider how holistic planning can help to meet the individual needs of a child who does not appear to be developing as expected:

- Can you describe how your planning will support the child's development?
- How will you ensure your planning takes account of their interests and benefits their learning?
- How might your planning help you to identify whether the child needs any additional support?
- What will your next steps be?

PLANNING IN THE MOMENT

The concept of child-centred practice and planning holistically can also be explored through a relatively new term – 'in the moment planning'. Many practitioners and indeed parents may feel this idea is not new, and it could be argued that it is an approach that has always existed in quality Early Years practice. In 2009 the Department for Children, Schools and Families introduced 'moment-by-moment' planning, which recommended that the skilful adult should always be ready to respond to children and plan for the 'next moment' (DCSF, 2009, p23). Planning in the moment, suggests Ephgrave (2018), is what any adult caring for children does 'every day'. It is about being respectful and inclusive and takes account of the way parents/carers and practitioners respond to children in a holistic way. Earlier in this chapter we talked about the importance of planning for children's individual needs. Planning in the moment does just that, as it enables the practitioner to respect the uniqueness of each individual child.

To explain further, the following account is taken from an interview with two undergraduate students currently in their second year of a BA Hons degree in Early Years.

CASE STUDY 2.2

Placement is an integral part of the degree course that Bethany and Ashlea are currently studying and they are both placed in school settings supporting children in Reception and following the EYFS framework.

Bethany and Ashlea talked about their experiences and in particular how their understanding of planning for children's needs had changed this year.

Bethany: *I think in the moment planning links to continuous provision. I have been encouraged to observe the children in my class and see what they are interested in. So,*

(Continued)

(Continued)

any ideas the children have, we can use them to take their learning further. This week one of the children was sitting with the class teacher talking about what they want to be in the future, and as the conversation developed one of the children said they wanted to be a scientist. As the excitement grew and other children joined in the teacher talked about science and experiments. The next day this was taken further, the children's interests were followed through and a range of 'experiments' were developed in the water, and with the paint, both in the inside and outdoor classroom. Recipes for potions were placed in the different areas for children to follow and read. The children became scientists, they wrote their own experiments, and this developed into telling stories of magic and spells.

Ashlea: *We have in the moment planning and it is managed in a way that makes sure all the children get a turn. We have a learning journey on the wall in the classroom. It starts the week blank but is completed by all the practitioners as they observe the children, and they add comments based on their observations. It really helps to involve parents too as there is an online app that parents can post to, so when they notice something out of school that their child is interested in they can let the staff know. It really helps the parents to feel involved. Parents can also talk to staff about their observations and these are added to the learning journey. At the end of each week the learning journey is full and everyone can see what learning has taken place.*

Both Bethany and Ashlea talked about the differences they have noticed this year. They also said they had found it hard to see initially how planning in this way rather than providing structured or adult directed activities helped children to learn. Both did say they are now converts, and really like the approach and feel they can see children take pride in what they are doing.

Bethany: *it really develops play.*

Ashlea: *the children are really happy in their play.*

When you plan in the moment, you also need to plan for the 'next steps', in the moment. As you are planning in the moment you will have been observing and assessing; then you plan how to take the children's interests one step further, in that moment, in order to enhance their learning and development. You will do this by reflecting-in-action (Schön, 1991), and while doing so, considering how you can enhance the activity at that moment in time. You will have to think on your feet and be alert and ready to respond. The Early Years National Strategies state,

Babies and young children are experiencing and learning in the here and now, not storing up their questions until tomorrow or next week. It is in that moment of curiosity, puzzlement, effort or interest – the 'teachable moment' – that the skilful adult makes a difference.

(DCSF, 2009, p23)

You will develop skills to become the 'skilful adult' and recognise and respond to the 'teachable moment'.

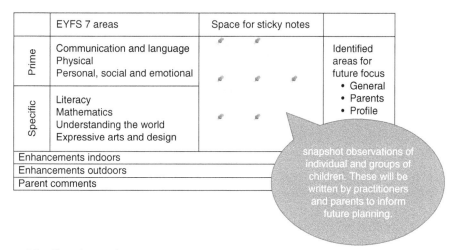

Figure 2.3 Planning tool

In Case study 2.2 Ashlea talks about contributing to children's learning through observations. She describes a learning journey on the classroom wall. The planning tool shown in Figure 2.3 was developed with Ashlea and Bethany's help – it is an example of a tool that can be used to enable you to plan for children's interests and can be used to support a collaborative approach to 'in the moment' planning. Ideally a small number of focus children will feature each week. Space is included to add snapshot observations written on sticky notes; these can be added by practitioners and parents/carers. Sections also allow for comments to be written about enhancements made during the week to the continuous provision both inside and out. Parents are encouraged to make general comments and give feedback and there are also prompts to encourage identified areas of focus and future planning.

When planning either after the event or in the moment, it is important to think about how you will scaffold children's learning and development, a concept introduced by Bruner. When scaffolding children's learning you are supporting them in developing their understanding of new concepts and tasks, where they will be actively engaged in their own learning through a rich dialogue between you and them (Dyer, 2017). The child should be an active participant in their learning and development and you must remember this throughout the observation, assessment and planning cycle.

FLEXIBILITY IN PLANNING

To ensure the principles of planning are effective, you need to maintain a flexible approach to planning. Sometimes you will plan activities or change provision; however, the children may not show particular interest or become engaged. Children are unpredictable and not always interested in what the adult plans. Their interests can change from day to day; just like adults, their moods can change and this impacts on what they want to do. If you have planned an activity and a particular child or group of children are not interested, you need to think about how you can change the activity to re-engage them. It may even be that you do not continue with the activity if children are disinterested; if children are disengaged they will not learn.

Don't be disheartened if this happens; we all learn through trial and error. Take time to reflect on why the children may have been disinterested and it may be that you need to observe again, as interests have changed. You should also talk to the children about why they may not have been interested and let them tell you what they would like to do. Through this type of dialogue, you can plan for activities you know they are interested in and develop an approach of sustained shared thinking.

CONCLUSION

This chapter introduced you to the principles of planning in the Early Years Foundation Stage and made particular reference to the *Development Matters* guidance (Early Education, 2012). Using theory and a range of examples it asked you to consider a number of ways that you can plan for children's individual needs. Working closely with parents is key to the principles of planning and making the links between the home environment and Nursery setting. The key person is integral to this approach and developing trusting relationships between practitioners and parents (Mukherji and Dryden, 2014; Crow and Froggett, 2017). Using this type of method in developing relationships clearly supports collaborative and inclusive approaches, and planning for children's individual care, learning and development needs. This must take into consideration Bronfenbrenner's (1979) human ecological model and you need to think about how children's immediate and wider influences may impact on their learning and development. It is also essential that you reflect on the stage that children are at and remember Piaget's pre-operational stage, where children aged 18 months to 6 years are very much concerned with their own experiences and perceptions of the world around them, not of others around them (Garhart Mooney, 2000). Every child is unique, and deserves to be supported by knowledgeable and confident practitioners who have their best interests at the heart of their practice.

FURTHER READING

Early Education (2012) *Development Matters in the Early Years Foundation Stage (EYFS)*. London: Early Education. Available online at: https://www.early-education.org.uk/development-matters-early-years-foundation-stage-eyfs-download

Ephgrave, A (2018) *Planning in the Moment with Young Children: A Practical Guide for Early Years Practitioners and Parents*. London: Routledge.

Hallet, E (2016) *Early Years Practice: For Educators and Teachers*. London: Sage.

REFERENCES

Arnold, C (2017) Sharing ideas with parents about key child development concepts, in Whalley, M and the Pen Green Centre Team (eds) *Involving Parents in their Children's Learning*. London: Sage.

Bronfenbrenner, U (1979) *The Ecology of Human Development*. Cambridge, MA: Harvard University Press.

Crow, A and Froggett, T (2017) Working with parents, in McMahon, S and Dyer, M (eds) *Work-Based Practice in the Early Years: A Guide for Students*. Abingdon: Routledge.

DCSF (2009) *Learning, Playing and Interacting Good Practice in the Early Years Foundation Stage*. Nottingham: DCSF Publications.

Department for Education (2017) *Statutory Framework for the Early Years Foundation Stage: Setting the Standards for Learning, Development and Care for Children from Birth to Five*. London: DfE.

Dyer, M (2017) How young children learn, in McMahon, S and Dyer, M (eds) *Work-Based Practice in the Early Years: A Guide for Students*. Abingdon: Routledge.

Early Education (2012) *Development Matters in the Early Years Foundation Stage (EYFS)*. London: Early Education. Available at https://www.foundationyears.org.uk/wp-content/uploads/2012/03/Development-Matters-FINAL-PRINT-AMENDED.pdf

Ephgrave, A (2018) *Planning in the Moment with Young Children: A Practical Guide for Early Years Practitioners and Parents*. London: Routledge.

Garhart Mooney, C (2000) *Theories of Childhood: An Introduction to Dewey, Montessori, Erikson, Piaget and Vygotsky*. St Paul, MN: Redleaf Press.

Hallet, E (2016) *Early Years Practice: For Educators and Teachers*. London: Sage.

Jackson, D and Needham, M (2014) *Engaging Parents with Early Years Settings*. London: Sage.

Keyte-Hartland, D (2018) Observation and the world of children's ideas. *Early Education Journal*, 84: 10–15.

Mukherji, P and Dryden, L (2014) *Foundations of Early Childhood: Principles and Practice*. London: Sage.

Schön, D (1991) *The Reflective Practitioner*. Aldershot: Ashgate Publishing.

3 OBSERVATION, ASSESSMENT AND THE PLANNING CYCLE

Samantha McMahon and Lindsey Watson

CHAPTER AIMS

By the end of this chapter you will be able to:

- consider the purposes of observation and assessment and how they support effective planning
- explore some of the different methods of observation and assessment, including digital
- examine some of the ethical challenges and issues of bias in observation and assessment
- consider how to interpret observations and use them in the planning process

As you read this chapter, refer to pages 6–46 (specifically, the column labelled 'A Unique Child') of *Development Matters in the Early Years Foundation Stage (EYFS)* (Early Education, 2012).

INTRODUCTION

It is only through accurate assessment that the practitioner understands children's achievements, interests and needs, and is able to plan for their next steps; assessment and planning begins with observation. This chapter considers some of the key features of effective assessment, explores types of assessment, and briefly touches upon some of the debates concerning assessment practice. To support practical and professional development the chapter includes some common methods of observation, including the use of ICT, and provides examples of how these might be interpreted and used in the assessment and planning cycle. The chapter draws attention to the importance of conducting accurate, ethical and holistic observations and assessments to ensure the focus is on capturing what a child is doing and can do, and not what they are not doing (Sancisi and Edgington, 2015).

ASSESSMENT

In beginning to think about assessment, a simple definition might help. Sancisi and Edgington (2015, p11) state 'an assessment is a judgement about the child's development and learning'. These judgments arise through reflection on and inter-pretation of one or more observations. In everyday practice, assessment might be understood as, practitioners knowing the children they work with, understanding their learning and being able to use this to plan for their progression (Dubiel, 2016).

ASSESSMENT IN THE EARLY YEARS FOUNDATION STAGE (EYFS)

The *Statutory Framework* (DfE, 2017, p13) describes *formative assessment* as ongoing assessment that involves practitioners observing children to understand their level of achievement, interests and learning styles to then shape learning experiences for each child. The EYFS also includes a requirement that *summative assessments* must be provided when a child is aged between 2 and 3, and that an EYFS Profile must be completed for each child in the final term of the year in which the child reaches age 5 (DfE, 2017). Summative assessment can be understood as the summary of achievement or attainment at a specific point in time and is derived from ongoing assessment (Dubiel, 2016).

THE PROGRESS CHECK AT AGE 2

It is required that practitioners provide a brief written summary, when a child is aged between 2 and 3, of their development in the prime areas, personal, social and emotional development, communication and language, and physical development. This check must identify the child's strengths and areas where their progress is less than expected, and the emphasis is on the need for early identification and inter-vention should there be any emerging concerns. The practitioner must include any activities or strategies they intend to adopt to support the child's future learning and development, including the involvement of other professionals. Parents should be included in providing information for the review and practitioners should take time to discuss the check with them including how it might be used in the home. Wherever possible it is intended that the progress check and the Healthy Child Programme Health and Development Review undertaken by the health visitor should inform each other, thus supporting a collaborative approach between health and education to meet the child's needs.

THE EARLY YEARS FOUNDATION STAGE PROFILE (EYFSP)

The EYFSP is completed by the Reception teacher towards the end of the summer term and the child's level of development must be assessed against the early learning goals. The teacher should indicate whether the child is *meeting, exceeding* or not yet meeting *(emerging)* expected levels of development. The profile must be shared with parents/carers and the Year 1 teacher and the intention is that it should 'provide parents and teachers with a well-rounded picture of the child's knowledge, under-standing and abilities, their progress against expected levels and their readiness for Year 1' (DfE, 2017, p14). This holistic picture of the child is drawn from ongoing observations, other records held by the setting, discussions with parents/carers and any other adults judged to offer a useful contribution. Schools are required to take part in EYFSP moderation events normally specified by the local authority (LA) and provide results of the EYFSP to the LA, who in turn have a duty to return this data to the government.

The EYFSP has a number of purposes including:

- informing parents/carers about their child's progress;
- supporting a smooth transition into Year 1 and to help Year 1 teachers plan an effective curriculum;
- providing data to evaluate the impact of the EYFS experience on children's outcomes and thus provide a means of accountability.

(Dubiel, 2016)

BASELINE ASSESSMENT

The type and format of summative assessment in Reception is set to change as the government announced its plans to introduce a statutory baseline assessment in autumn 2020. It is intended that this assessment will be undertaken by the teacher soon after the pupils enter Reception. It will assess children's abilities in:

- communication, language and literacy;
- early mathematical skills;
- self-regulation (although this is to be confirmed).

The assessment will last approximately 20 minutes and the government stresses that it is being introduced to support school-level progress measures which show the progress pupils make from Reception to the end of Key Stage 2, and it will eventually replace the existing EYFSP and assessments at Key Stage 1 (DfE, 2018). Such one off decontextualised summative assessments early in the school year can be criticised for the partial picture of the child that is collected, having little use for the teacher in supporting their planning for the child's learning and development, and crucially for taking the teacher away from teaching and getting to know the children in their class. The key principle of this type of assessment is accountability and measuring school effectiveness; however, scoring children in such assessments is difficult to manage practically and ethically, as children can find it stressful when required to 'perform' on a particular day. There are also concerns about how the assessment will be tailored for children with specific needs and challenges, and for the very youngest summer born children.

REFLECTION ACTIVITY 3.1

Research arguments both for and against baseline assessment and compare with those for and against EYFSP. Reflect on which is most useful to parents, practitioners and the child.

Useful sources of information:

Roberts-Holmes, G and Bradbury, A (2016) Governance, accountability and the datafication of early years education in England, *British Educational Research Journal*, 42 (4): 600–13.

Berliner, W (2018) Proposed tests for reception children 'verging on the immoral'. Online www.theguardian.com/education/2018/jan/16/tests-reception-children-immoral-england-play

Consider what the practitioner needs to know about the child in the first six weeks in a setting in order to plan for their learning and development needs, and the best way of gathering this information.

In order for practitioners to meet their responsibilities in planning for children's learning and development accurate ongoing formative assessment is key.

FROM ASSESSMENT TO PLANNING

To ensure this chapter reflects 'real life' practice I spent some time in Reception with the class teacher, Miriam, discussing how assessment informs her planning. Some of the planning, particularly for phonics and maths, required her to follow school schemes. There would be a whole class starter activity on the carpet followed by differentiated activities tailored to the child's assessed level of development. Miriam and her team understand the children's learning and development needs from ongoing formative assessment, that is observations they have recorded via an app. The differentiated follow-on activities are called 'superhero' activities and every child has their own superhero sign, a generic superhero template with the child's photograph on, and they go to the activity where their superhero sign is located. Throughout the week children have opportunities to work on adult led activities and to consolidate their learning through play in the continuous provision. Miriam also used the assessments to reflect on provision more generally in the setting and recognised that opportunities for expressive arts and design were limited and children's learning and development in this area was not progressing. Therefore, she adapted her planning to include more art and design, both indoors and outdoors, and encouraged the children to experiment with mixing paint and making their own art from found natural materials. The children particularly enjoyed making art outside and when the snow fell covering their work they thought it was lost, only to be amazed when it melted several days later and their art was still there. Magic!

Miriam draws inspiration for her planning from many places and adapts ideas she finds on the internet; however, she stressed that she was constantly reviewing her planning in response to the children's holistic learning and development needs. Miriam uses ongoing formative assessment to plan effectively, which relies on regular and accurate observation.

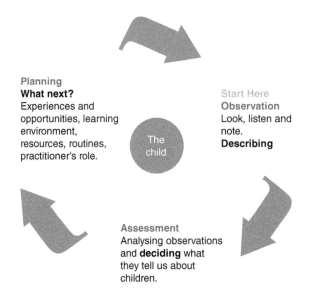

Planning
What next?
Experiences and opportunities, learning environment, resources, routines, practitioner's role.

The child

Start Here
Observation
Look, listen and note.
Describing

Assessment
Analysing observations and **deciding** what they tell us about children.

Figure 3.1   Observation, assessment and planning (Early Education, 2012, p3)

OBSERVATION

Development Matters (Early Education 2012, p3) clearly articulates the central place of observation in the assessment and planning cycle below.

In Figure 3.1 the starting point for *observation* is to look, listen and note, and these observations should then be analysed. The analysis can begin by considering the examples of development listed in each area of learning in *Development Matters*, in the columns headed A Unique Child. This helps the practitioner and student identify where the child is in their developmental pathway, *assessment*. The next step is to use the assessment to *plan* experiences and learning opportunities to strengthen and deepen the child's learning and development. This can be done by reflecting on the guidance provided in *Development Matters* in each area of learning in the columns headed Positive Relationships and Enabling Environments. Practitioners are expected to develop many approaches to supporting children's learning and development but these columns are a useful starting point, particularly for less experienced practitioners and students. In addition, practitioners will also want to assess the child's disposition to learning, that is the way they approach and engage with people and the environment. Therefore, they will analyse the observation to see how the child demonstrates the characteristics of effective learning (CoEL), playing and exploring, active learning and creating and thinking critically (Early Education, 2012, p5).

REFLECTION ACTIVITY 3.2

Spend some time familiarising yourself with the CoEL as set out on pages 5, 6 and 7 in *Development Matters*. Consider what adults can do and what they might provide in order to support the child in developing a positive disposition to learning.

HOW TO OBSERVE

As a student or inexperienced practitioner it can be challenging to know how to observe children and begin the assessment and planning process. Sancisi and Edgington (2015) describe the observation process as capturing the facts of what we see the child do and what we hear the child say. Observing is a skill which you can practise by taking every opportunity to quickly jot down in a notebook or on a sticky note what you have seen and heard the child do and say. In many settings, observations are recorded on a range of digital devices using an app or a bespoke software package and this is covered later in the chapter.

✓ TIPS FOR PRACTICE

As a student you may not initially be confident or allowed to use technology to observe, so I recommend that you keep a notebook to hand and regularly observe a child for five minutes, writing down what you see and hear. Make a note of the child's age in

(Continued)

(Continued)

months, their gender and any other relevant information which might influence their behaviour, for example the presence of other children and adults. By regularly undertaking these short narrative style observations you will:

- build confidence
- acquire observational skills
- get to know the children
- extend your knowledge and understanding of how children learn and develop
- enhance your understanding of the EYFS in practice

Narrative observations are useful in practice because generally the adult is not involved and they focus on child-initiated play and so provide the practitioner with an opportunity to see the child as they really are. Miriam ensures that regular narrative observations are undertaken on the tablet so that each child is looked at closely for their characteristics of effective learning, and in respect of their holistic development. There are other methods of observation summarised below but those most often used in practice alongside narrative are snapshot/spontaneous observation and participant observation.

Snapshots or spontaneous observations are a brief record of what the child is doing and Sancisi and Edgington (2015) suggest that the practitioner must have eyes and ears everywhere so that they notice what needs noticing. They also suggest that it may need acting on immediately, leading to spontaneous planning, so that the observation and planning are recorded retrospectively. To understand how observations can lead to spontaneous planning or planning in the moment I visited Felicity, the manager of a pre-school. Drawing on a recent example, she explained how some of the older children aged from 36–48 months had been talking about the royal wedding and one girl said her mum was making a cake. This led to experimenting with making different types of cakes from playdough where the girl talked about inviting people to a party to eat the cake. At circle time the practitioner asked if the other children would like to have a party and who they would invite. The children decided they would like to invite parents and the children from Reception in the neighbouring school. It was decided to go ahead with the party and the practitioners were able to link the related activities such as making decorations, baking cakes and writing invitations to literacy, maths, understanding the world and to supporting transition into school. All the planning for these activities came from the children and was written up retrospectively.

Another example of spontaneous planning, Spring, came from observing two of the children looking at the lambs in the field. Felicity explained that this type of planning could be challenging, *'it's messy, I'm lucky I have great staff who know the children really well and are confident, they're on board, less experienced staff might struggle'*. She also explained that the staff know the children really well and this is because of the way the key person system works in the setting. Felicity said, *'the child chooses their Key Person, we observe them for a few weeks once they have started the setting to see which member of staff they are most comfortable with'*. Each key person works closely with the parents and regularly observes the child; this information is recorded in the child's learning journey, a detailed record that includes observations and photographs of the child in the setting and at home, and parents are encouraged to contribute. The staff team meet regularly and share what they know about their key children, and to write up the planning. This way all of the staff know the children.

Read the case study below, which provides an example of a snapshot or spontaneous observation that led to spontaneous planning.

CASE STUDY 3.1

Karen observed a group of children playing in the small world, racing cars. As the space was tight Karen wondered whether she might extend their learning and enjoyment by asking if they would like to build a race track outside using crates and guttering. The children were really excited by this and became engrossed in designing and building the race track. They had to work collaboratively and test out how to make the structure stable. Karen found some books on bridges in the book corner and one of the children remembered paying money at a bridge on holiday. The children worked on the structure over several days constructing a complex track with ramps at different angles and a toll bridge.

From this case study what have you learnt about snapshot/spontaneous observations and planning? Are there any challenges? You might reflect on the skill of the practitioner and their ability to sensitively scaffold the children's learning, and the availability of resources.

In practice you might also undertake participant observations which means that you are working with the child and make a note of something significant in their development. It might be something you have not seen the child do before, or something interesting they have said. Sometimes this significant moment can be captured in a photograph, other times it might just be a brief note on a sticky note. There are a number of ways to observe as shown in Table 3.1.

Table 3.1   Methods of observation

Observation methods	Advantages	Disadvantages
Time sample Observe a child for a brief amount of time, e.g. for 1 minute at regular intervals, e.g. 10 minutes during a session.	Useful to capture data about a child you are concerned about or to discover which equipment or areas of provision are being accessed.	Time consuming. Observer might lose concentration and miss a recording.
Event sample (sometimes referred to as ABC) A log is completed over as long a period of time as possible to capture particular types of behaviour.	Can reveal underlying causes or patterns of behaviour, specifically what came before the behaviour, **A**ntecedent, what occurred, **B**ehaviour and what happened as a result of the behaviour, **C**onsequences.	Allocating time. The expected behaviour may not occur during the time allocated to observe. Making it obvious to the child that they are being observed.

(Continued)

Table 3.1   (Continued)

Observation methods	Advantages	Disadvantages
Checklist/Ticklist A pre-prepared list of developmental milestones, or children's skills to be ticked off when observed.	Quick. User friendly and easily repeated. Results are obvious and readily understandable.	Checklists may not give a true picture, e.g if the child is unwell or feels they are being tested. Challenging to maintain objectivity if you believe a child has previously achieved a milestone.
Longitudinal study Takes place over a period of time and may consist of a number of different types of observation. Students may be required to complete this type of study to closely record a child's progress over time. Sometimes known as a child's learning journey.	Provides detailed insight into the individual and unique child. Can reveal how effectively the environment is supporting the child's learning and development. Can be shared and enjoyed by parents, children and staff.	The child might leave the setting, or become ill. Your observations might upset parents, particularly if they show atypical development or behaviour.
Target child A pre-coded observation usually to study concentration and interaction.	Allows the observer to focus clearly on one specific aspect of development. Shows how the setting promotes language development.	Time consuming. Codes need to be learned and practised before use.

Adapted from McMahon, 2017.

DIGITAL TECHNOLOGY

This section considers the role of digital technologies within the observation process. Over recent years, educators and policymakers have highlighted the potential possibilities of digital technologies to transform aspects of pedagogical practices within the early childhood education sector as a way of supporting the assessment of children's learning and development (Blackwell et al., 2014). In a contemporary context, the term digital technologies in relation to assessment potentially relates to a range of devices, including but not limited to, internet enabled computers, mobile phones, cameras and tablets (Arnott, 2016). One way that these changes have been incorporated into effective practice is the increasing use of digital technologies to improve the observation process.

Initially, it is important that the pedagogical limitations of these digital technologies are understood. The evidence collected using digital technologies does not replace other forms of assessment, such as narrative or participant observations (previously discussed); rather, they are used to enhance the process. Related to the notion of the unique child, photos and videos offer the chance to collect holistic objective accounts of children's learning and development, providing evidence of what the child can do (Palaiologou, 2016). The use of digital technologies can often save practitioners time and offer opportunities for secure information sharing with parents. However, it is not the technology alone that supports the pedagogy, but also the practitioner's knowledge, understanding and interpretations of child development that allows for effective assessment for learning (Blackwell et al., 2014).

Another pedagogical consideration is that digital observation techniques allow young children more opportunities to be involved in the observation process. Eaude (2011) identifies the importance of young children assessing and steering their own learning, being active participants which in turn supports their intrinsic motivation. Digital technology provides younger children with the tools to share in the responsibility of the observation process, increasing their agency and voice, allowing them to become co-constructors of knowledge in the matters that are important to them (Fleet et al., 2017).

Practitioners often welcome the flexibility offered by the use of digital technologies. There are a growing number of online interactive systems and APPs commercially available, meaning there are multiple opportunities to carry out, record, assess and share children's learning journeys. These online interactive systems include digital storage, which saves physical space and offers specific file sharing where needed. Similarly, those wanting to view an array of information, such as a practitioner looking at observations of a child over a long period of time to track their progress, or a parent wanting to view their child's engagement at a setting, can do so.

Ethical use of digital technologies within the observation process must be considered. The General Data Protection Regulation (GDPR) law, introduced in May 2018, includes six privacy principles that practitioners should consider when collecting and sharing observational data of children (Pre-School Learning Alliance, 2017).

- When collecting data, this must be done in a fair and transparent way.
- The data must only be used for the reason it was initially obtained.
- Settings must only collect data that is necessary.
- Data must be accurate and up to date.
- Data must not be kept longer than is necessary.

Settings are accountable for their compliance in managing data, training staff and updating policies in terms of data protection (Pre-School Learning Alliance, 2017). All online interactive assessment systems are also accountable to the GDPR law, which is aimed at increasing privacy and protection around personal data.

Practitioners' pre-existing beliefs, perceptions and confidence with technology can impact on their attitudes towards the use of digital devices within their practice (Chua and Chua, 2016; Ertmer et al., 2012). Also considered is the lack of access to technology, such as time for training or professional development opportunities. This suggests practitioners potentially face multiple barriers around the decisions to adopt digital technologies within the early childhood education environment, including agentic barriers around their own personal views and structural considerations impacted by a lack of continued professional development opportunities (Parette et al., 2010; Wachira and Keengwe, 2010). Those practitioners who are more comfortable around technology are more likely to use it in their practice (Karaca et al., 2013). Considering the cost of digital devices, sufficient training for practitioners is paramount to make sure they are confident digital users. This is aimed at ensuring settings get the most from incorporating digital technology into their practice, which in turn has the potential to have a beneficial impact on assessing children's learning and development.

BIAS IN OBSERVATIONS

Whatever method of observation is used it is essential that it is accurate, which in turn should support accurate assessment of children's learning and development. Dubiel (2016) calls for observation and assessment to be authentic, real, honest and accurate.

REFLECTION ACTIVITY 3.3 (ADAPTED FROM DUBIEL, 2016)

If a child has been inaccurately observed and is judged to be at a higher level of development than they actually are, what are the potential consequences for the child?

While it is unlikely that one inaccurate observation would lead to harmful consequences for the child's learning and development, practitioners should adopt an approach to observation that minimises the chance of bias.

Hobart and Frankel (2004) remind practitioners that during observations they are likely to make judgements based on their own cultural values, and their upbringing and experiences; however, many of the children they observe may have been brought up in a different culture. Their families may have very different expectations of children's behaviour and this may affect how they play and relate to other children and adults in the setting. In some cultures, it is considered disrespectful to look an adult in the eye and some parents may hold strong views on gender and appropriate types of play. It can be useful to try and develop your understanding of other cultures to lessen the chance of cultural bias. Observations are also affected by our first impressions of a child, particularly of dominant characteristics such as how chatty and friendly they are, and we can then unwittingly distort our observations to fit these first impressions (McMahon, 2017). Similarly, prior knowledge of a child's family can affect how we interpret observations.

REFLECTION ACTIVITY 3.4

As a student you may be asked to undertake observations of specific children. Imagine that you are asked to observe a child and are told that you are observing because there are concerns about the child's behaviour and that it appears he is following in the footsteps of his older brother who was always in trouble, and that it is not surprising because the whole family are a 'nightmare', often at the centre of trouble on the local housing estate.

What impression might you form of this child and his family? Consider how this might affect your approach to the observation.

✓ **TIPS FOR PRACTICE**

To minimise bias

- only record what you see and hear
- use objective neutral language
- observe regularly, use different methods to observe
- discuss observations with other practitioners
- compare your observations with observations of the same child by other practitioners

ETHICAL PRACTICE

By adopting an approach to observations that minimises bias you are demonstrating respectful and ethical practice. Ethical practice also includes securing informed consent from parents to observe their children and ensuring that all data is stored securely. As a student you will anonymise all observations to protect the identity of the child, their family and practitioners. Wherever possible the child should also consent to being observed although in practice parental consent is normally considered to be sufficient. Harvell and McMahon (2016) argue that the very act of observation can disturb a child's feelings and change their behaviour; therefore, students and practitioners should be alert to verbal and non-verbal cues that indicate that a child does not want to be observed. This is particularly important in very young children and children who are unable to speak.

INTERPRETING OBSERVATIONS

In practice when interpreting observations and planning for a child's learning you will normally be able to take account of their interests and preferred way of learning; it is not possible in this section to provide this detail. Nevertheless, the observation set out in Table 3.2 can support you in reflecting on how the child learns, focusing on the CoEL, making links to *Development Matters* and planning their next steps. A detailed discussion of how the observation was interpreted and used to plan the next steps for Finton is set out below the observation.

In completing the observation proforma in Table 3.2, initially focusing on his strengths and interests, it appears that Finton enjoyed playing and experimenting with the water. He also seemed to like collaborating and playing with Ben and was willing to be guided in his learning by the practitioner. Then we turn to *Development Matters* for evidence of significant learning; however, do not expect one observation to provide evidence in every area and remember, on its own it is difficult to judge what is significant for Finton. The information collected in this observation would be more significant if we knew for example that he had recently started at the setting and had not made friends, or that Finton had not been observed using talk to communicate ideas. Even though the information presented in this observation is limited, our interpretations contribute to ongoing formative assessment of the child.

Table 3.2 Example observation: Finton

OBSERVATION	
Name of child: Finton, age: 38 mths	Observed by: Sam
Date: 26/3/2017	Learning context:
	water tray, indoors, 1
adult/2ch	

Finton is standing by the water tray; he reaches over and takes the jug from Ben, Ben says 'hey that's mine'. Finton looks at Ben and then at the nearby practitioner who says 'you could give that jug to Ben and get one from the shelf'. Finton looks at Ben and hands him the jug, then takes another from the shelf; he leans over the water tray and fills the jug, brings it to his mouth and tastes the water, then pours it into the tray. Ben says 'pour it here', pointing to his full jug. Finton refills his jug and pours it into Ben's which overflows and splashes them both. They laugh and Ben says 'fill yours and I'll crash mine'. Finton fills his jug and holds it in the tray, Ben fills his, then bumps it into Finton's. Water splashes, both boys laugh. 'Now mine' says Finton and both boys fill their jugs and Finton crashes his into Ben's, the water splashes and the boys laugh. The practitioner comes over and says 'boys, try and keep the water in the tray'. Finton looks at Ben and says 'it's a wave' and Ben looks at the practitioner then Finton and says 'we're making a flood aren't we?' Finton nods. The practitioner says 'oh okay but it's slippery, so how about we look for different ways to make waves. What's on the shelf?' Both boys go to the shelf, Finton picks up a tube, brings it to his eye and then blows down it on Ben's face. Ben says 'hey it's the wind'. He picks up a tube and both boys return to the water tray and start blowing it. The practitioner says 'maybe try with a boat'. She hands them three different sized boats and the boys blow them on the water. Finton says 'it's a race'.

Evidence of significant learning:

PSED	CL	PD	L	UW	M	EAD
30–50						

Characteristics of effective learning:

Playing and exploring: Finton is willing to have a go at the activities proposed by Ben and the practitioner. Also when he lifts the tube to his eye perhaps he is investigating what it can do.

Active learning: Finton spends 5 minutes at the end blowing the boats; this demonstrates concentration.

Creating and thinking critically: Finton shows that he can **think critically** when he makes links between blowing the water making waves, and the boats racing.

Next Steps: I want Finton to be more confident in communicating with children and adults in social situations. I will build on his interest in racing the boats in the water tray by taking them outside and using large tubes, drain pipes and resources selected by Finton. We will plan and build a boat as a group and investigate floating, sinking and how boats are propelled in the water, boat races?

This observation might tell us something about Finton's personal, social, emotional development (PSED), communication and language development (CL), understanding the world (UW) and possibly physical development (PD). This example will focus on PSED. Turning to *Development Matters*, page 9, refer to the Unique Child at 30–50 months to see if any of the statements apply to Finton. There is some evidence that Finton can play in a group, at least with one other child, and that he keeps play going when he responds to Ben and the practitioner. Towards the end of the observation he does seem to initiate the conversation and does demonstrate friendly behaviour. Therefore, for PSED-Making Relationships, Finton seems to be meeting the expected level of development for a child aged 30–50 months. Moving to PSED: self-confidence and self-awareness at 30–50 months, page 11, the observation does not provide much evidence for this aspect of PSED; at most we might judge that he is able to select and use resources with help. Turning to page 13 for the next aspect of PSED: Managing feelings and behaviour at 30–50 months, there is evidence that Finton begins to accept the needs of others, take turns and share resources sometimes with support from others. He gave the jug back to Ben when asked and took his turn in pouring and crashing the jugs. He was also able to adapt his behaviour when asked by the practitioner; together these suggest he is meeting some aspects of this area of PSED. Therefore, on balance we might indicate on the observation sheet that for PSED he is at 30–50 months. This process would be repeated for the appropriate areas of learning and development. These judgements are supported by then referring to the characteristics of effective learning.

Recognising how children demonstrate the CoEL takes skill and confidence accrued through experience, so initially it can be challenging. However, in the observation of Finton there is evidence of *playing and exploring* – he is willing to have a go at the activities proposed by Ben and the practitioner. Also when he lifts the tube to his eye perhaps he is investigating what it can do. When Finton and Ben spend five minutes at the end blowing the boats, this demonstrates concentration and *active learning*, and Finton shows that he can *think critically* when he makes links between blowing the water making waves, and the boats racing.

Ideally, to identify the next steps for Finton you would have a number of observations to be able to set a clear learning priority (Sancisi and Edgington, 2015). Sancisi and Edgington (2015) refer to a learning priority rather than next steps to avoid viewing children's learning and development like a ladder where children are made to constantly climb the next rung. Children often need to spend time consolidating their learning before moving on to the next step. For the purposes of this example you might want to consider the area of PSED where there is evidence of less progress, self-confidence and self-awareness. To write the learning priority or next step, use clear language from the relevant section, A Unique Child, in *Development Matters*, e.g. I want Finton to be more confident in communicating with children and adults in social situations. Then write how you will do this, perhaps building on his interest in racing the boats in the water tray. This activity could be enhanced by being taken outside and experimenting with a range of different tubes and boats, and including other children. You might support Finton by helping him choose the resources, inviting children to take part, or supporting him in building a boat or investigating what else could be used to propel the boats on the water. Remember, *Development Matters* is not a checklist and children do not have to achieve every point in a band. In practice, priority is often on the prime areas of development for the next steps but over time children must have access to all areas of learning and development.

REFLECTION ACTIVITY 3.5

Using the observation of Lydia set out in Table 3.3, have a go at interpreting the data to plan her learning priority or next steps. Consider what the observation tells us about Lydia's strengths and interests, then turn to *Development Matters*, initially focusing on the prime areas, to identify the appropriate level of development. Then turn to the CoEL to reflect on her disposition as a learner and consider what you might plan as her next learning priority or next step.

Table 3.3   Example observation: Lydia

OBSERVATION	
Name of child: Lydia, age: 30 mths	Observed by: Sam
Date: 26/3/2014	Learning context:
	indoors, sensory room, 1
adult/2ch	

L is standing by the bubble tube watching herself in the mirror and singing as she points to her nose 'I can nose, nose', she kisses the tube and sings 'shoulders, knees and toes'. The practitioner says 'are you singing head, shoulders, knees and toes?'. Lydia smiles then puts her head down, jumps down, runs to Alfie and falls over. Lydia says 'fall down'; she looks around, gets up, brushes down her dress and says 'fall down'. Lydia walks to Alfie and picks up a foam tube which she uses to hit the light panel on the wall progressively harder and harder, then throws down the tube. Alfie moves away from the light panel and Lydia moves with him to the platform with the bubble tube. Lydia moves round the tube and follows a bubble with her finger; she peers from behind the tube and laughs, then goes back behind the tube and jumps out from the tube at Alfie who laughs, Lydia laughs. Lydia and Alfie then take it in turns playing peekaboo around the tube for 3 minutes. Alfie then touches Lydia's head and face, Lydia smiles then laughs. They both jump down from the platform touch heads and laugh. Lydia and Alfie run into the soft area and Lydia picks up a tube and when Alfie looks down the other end she sings 'shoulders, knees and toes'. Lydia runs to the practitioner, grabs her hand and says 'wee wee', the practitioner takes Lydia's hand and says 'oh well done you need the toilet'.

Evidence of significant learning:						
PSED	CL	PD	L	UW	M	EAD

Characteristics of effective learning:

Next Steps:

When interpreting observations and planning children's learning priorities, you should include their:

- interests;
- dispositions, how they approach learning as evidenced by the CoEL;
- relationships;
- feelings;
- skills;
- access to areas of learning and development;
- progress.

CONCLUSION

Observation and assessment are at the heart of effective planning in the EYFS and all three require skill, confidence and knowledge of child development. Therefore, it is essential to take every opportunity to practise and reflect with your mentor and colleagues on your observations, assessments and planning. Furthermore, check that your practice is ethical and your observations are free from bias; involve parents and children in the process and be creative. Planning is important but remember to act in the moment if you see a child struggling with something. Give support – this will involve observing, assessing, interpreting and identifying the learning need and acting on it. You may be able to record this after the fact but it is not necessary to document every aspect of practice.

FURTHER READING

Brodie, K (2013) *Observation, Assessment and Planning in the Early Years: Bringing It All Together.* Maidenhead: Open University Press.

REFERENCES

Arnott, L (2016) The role of digital technologies, in Palaiologou, I (ed) *The Early Years Foundation Stage: Theory and Practice.* London: Sage, pp329–41.

Blackwell, C K, Lauricella, A R and Wartella, E (2014) Factors influencing digital technology use in early childhood education. *Computers & Education, 77:* 82–90.

Chua, M and Chua, C (2016) App characteristics guide for ICT integration in early childhood education: an experience analysis. Paper presented at the 28th Australian Conference on Computer–Human Interaction. Launceston, Tasmania.

Department for Education (2017) *Statutory Framework for the Early Years Foundation Stage: Setting the Standards for Learning, Development and Care for Children from Birth to Five.* London: DfE.

Dubiel, J (2016) *Effective Assessment in the Early Years Foundation Stage* (2nd edn). London: Sage.

Early Education (2012) *Development Matters in the Early Years Foundation Stage (EYFS).* London: Early Education. Available at https://www.foundationyears.org.uk/wp-content/uploads/2012/03/Development-Matters-FINAL-PRINT-AMENDED.pdf

Eaude, T (2011) *Thinking Through Pedagogy for Primary and Early Years.* London: Sage.

Ertmer, P A, Ottenbreit-Leftwich, A T, Sadik, O, Sendurur, E and Sendurur, P (2012) Teachers' beliefs and technology integration practices: a critical relationship. *Computers & Education, 59*(2): 423–35. http://dx.doi.org/10.1016/j.compedu.2012.02.001.

Fleet, A, Patterson, C and Robertson, J (2017) *Pedagogical Documentation in Early Years Practice: Seeing Through Multiple Perspectives.* Thousand Oaks, CA: Sage.

Harvell, J and McMahon, S (2016) *Observation in The Early Years Handbook for Students and Practitioners: An Essential Guide for the Foundation Degree and Levels 4 and 5.* Abingdon: Routledge, pp403–15.

Hobart, C and Frankel, J (2004) *A Practical Guide to Child Observation and Assessment* (3rd edn). Cheltenham: Nelson Thornes.

Karaca, F, Can, G and Yildirim, S (2013) A path model for technology integration into elementary school settings in Turkey. *Computers & Education, 68:* 353–65.

McMahon, S (2017) Observation and assessment, in McMahon, S and Dyer, M (eds) *Work-Based Practice in the Early Years: A Guide for Students.* London: Routledge, pp108–20.

Palaiologou, I (2016) *Child Observation: A Guide for Students of Early Childhood.* London: Sage.

Parette, H P, Quesenberry, A C and Blum, C (2010) Missing the boat with technology usage in early childhood settings: a 21st century view of developmentally appropriate practice. *Early Childhood Education Journal, 37*(5): 335–43.

Pre-School Learning Alliance (2017) *Preparing Your Early Years Setting for GDPR.* Available at www.pre-school.org.uk/preparing-your-early-years-setting-gdpr (accessed 23 May 2018).

Sancisi, L and Edgington, M (2015) *Developing High Quality Observation, Assessment and Planning in the Early Years: Made to Measure.* Abingdon: Routledge.

Wachira, P and Keengwe, J (2010) Technology integration barriers: urban school mathematics teachers' perspectives. *Journal of Science Education and Technology, 20:* 17–25.

SECTION 2

PLANNING FOR LEARNING

4 PLANNING FOR THE PRIME AREAS OF LEARNING

Samantha McMahon and Jo McEvoy

CHAPTER AIMS

By the end of this chapter you will:

- be familiar with the content and purpose of the prime areas of learning, personal social and emotional development, physical development and communication and language, as outlined in *Development Matters* (Early Education, 2012)
- appreciate why the prime areas of learning underpin all other areas of learning and development in the EYFS
- know how to plan for children's learning and development in the prime areas through an enabling environment and positive adult–child relationships

As you read this chapter, refer to pages 8–27 of *Development Matters in the Early Years Foundation Stage (EYFS)* (Early Education, 2012).

INTRODUCTION

All areas of learning and development are interconnected and each area of development is affected by the other. However, for ease of understanding and so that parents and practitioners can articulate developmental patterns (Neaum, 2013), development can be divided into areas. Three areas have been identified in the EYFS as particularly 'crucial for igniting children's curiosity and enthusiasm for learning, and for building their capacity to learn, form relationships and thrive' (DfE, 2017, p7). These prime areas are:

- personal, social and emotional development;
- physical development;
- communication and language.

PERSONAL, SOCIAL AND EMOTIONAL DEVELOPMENT (PSED)

Langston (2014, p83) explains that PSED 'centres on the child's attitudes to themselves and others and to events, experiences and activities as well as their beliefs about their own ability and about learning itself'. Children's attitudes and beliefs about themselves are shaped by significant close relationships and social interactions. Bowlby's theory of attachment (1969, 1988) has been instrumental in shaping understanding and practice in supporting children's PSED, particularly his idea that the caring interactions between the child and their primary care giver are fundamental to the child's understanding of relationships and how to behave in them. Manning-Morton (2014) explains that babies and young children who experience loving responses to their signals develop mental concepts that adults can be trusted and the child feels valued and worthwhile. The importance of the adult's loving response to the child's signals is recognised in the EYFS (DfE, 2017, p22) which states every child must be assigned a key person – this is a special person in the setting that builds a relationship with the child.

THE KEY PERSON

The key person, ideally, should be chosen by the child as described by Felicity in Chapter 3; however, this is not the case in many settings. Nevertheless, the key person must create a special relationship with the child, welcoming them warmly to the setting and taking time to get to know them. The Nursery experience is very different from the home experience and the child will be exposed to unfamiliar sounds, smells, routines, food and people; this transition can be very unsettling for the child and they need a caring and sensitive adult to support them. Transitions, particularly starting a new setting, can also be challenging for parents, and the key person should build a special relationship with the parents; this will help allay fears at transition, and once the child is settled supports a strong partnership between the practitioner, parents and child.

REFLECTION ACTIVITY 4.1

In your setting how is the key person allocated to the child? Does this system work for the child, parents and the practitioners? How is information shared between parents, key person and the child, and is it reflected in the planning?

THREE ASPECTS OF PERSONAL, SOCIAL AND EMOTIONAL DEVELOPMENT

There are three aspects to this prime area of learning:

- making relationships;
- self-confidence and self-awareness;
- managing feelings and behaviour.

The key person has an important part to play in each of these aspects of PSED; this section considers each in turn.

Making relationships

Babies and young children base their understanding of relationships on those they experience in the home and in the setting. The key person must have time to bond with their key child and to get to know their likes and dislikes, and to understand their needs. Over time they also need to ensure that the child has opportunities to join in with other children and practitioners. The key person will model considerate and responsive interactions and help their key child understand their feelings. It is important that the planning incorporates time for the child to be with their key person individually, in a key group, with the rest of the group and other practitioners.

REFLECTION ACTIVITY 4.2

It is important that the environment in the setting supports 'making relationships'. Consider whether there are areas that allow children to sit and snuggle with their key person or friends to chat, read a story, or look at photos? Which resources promote cooperation and reflect an inclusive ethos?

Self-confidence and self-awareness

Developing self-confidence and self-awareness is a process that begins with children experiencing unconditional love and positive regard in their earliest attachments (Langston 2014), including their key person. The key person provides a secure base, physically and emotionally for the child to explore and actively engage with the environment.

✓ TIPS FOR PRACTICE

The key person can help children become self-confident and develop self-awareness by:

- offering praise and recognition for effort, rather than achievement, e.g. I can see you tried really hard to put your coat on by yourself, well done, would you like some help to do your zipper?
- finding and celebrating their key child's uniqueness, e.g. incorporating their knowledge of and interest in dinosaurs into the planning
- talking about the things they can do and are learning to do
- sharing photographs of the child, making a special book with them about them, including why they are special and what makes their family special
- celebrating special days and events, e.g. becoming a big sister or brother

(Adapted from Langston, 2014, p87)

Managing feelings and behaviour

The key person can help the child manage their emotions by offering them reassurance and support when they are upset and distressed and by talking about their feelings. Planning can include stories, use of persona dolls, pictures and music to help children consider feelings. By consistently modelling considerate and respectful behaviour and setting clear boundaries children begin to understand appropriate behaviour. This can be positively reinforced, for example, 'Liam you were kind when you let Adam have a turn on the bike, especially as he was sad when his mummy left'. The key person can also involve the child in finding solutions to problems and conflicts.

REFLECTION ACTIVITY 4.3

Take time to read the setting's behaviour policy; how is it shared with the children and parents, and is it implemented consistently in the setting?

PHYSICAL DEVELOPMENT

Goodsir (2016) points out that students often lack confidence in supporting children's physical development perhaps because of concerns over health and safety, lack of knowledge and their own negative experiences of physical education. *Development Matters* is a useful starting point for students to extend their knowledge and understanding of physical development as the statements reflect typical development for a specific age range. Also remember babies and young children love being active as they explore, communicate and build relationships through their bodies, and take great delight in learning new skills and showing what their bodies can do.

TWO ASPECTS OF PHYSICAL DEVELOPMENT

There are two aspects to this prime area of learning:

- moving and handling;
- health and self-care.

Moving and handling

This aspect of physical development describes the progress of children's control over their body and is cumulative, that is, from simple to complex, each stage building on a previous stage. Babies are born with a number of reflexes to ensure survival – startle, grasp, stepping, sucking and rooting – that appear to act as templates for later movements; they also have a well-developed sense of smell, touch, taste and hearing which enables them to explore their surroundings (Goodsir, 2016). Also at birth, the baby's brain has billions of neurons in place that require feeling and movement and sensori-motor experiences to become connected (DoH, 2011). Therefore, physical activity should be encouraged from birth and a variety of resources and experiences that stimulate babies' senses should be provided. Goodsir (2016, p255) refers to 'tummy time' for non-walking babies whereby the baby is positioned on their stomach which helps strengthen muscles in the arms, legs and neck, and assists head control. It also supports later skills such as rolling, crawling and eventually walking.

✓ TIPS FOR PRACTICE

Although tummy time can be used with very young babies it should be kept short, 1–2 minutes maximum, and it is important to be alert to the baby becoming distressed. If this happens, stop, give the baby a cuddle and try again the next day, gradually building up the time they spend on their front.

REFLECTION ACTIVITY 4.4

Research floor-based activities you can provide for non-walking babies to support their physical development. Then consider how you might adapt the environment for the young child as they learn to sit unsupported and then become more independent as they start to crawl.

Useful resources include:

Development Matters, page 22

British Heart Foundation (2013) *Early Movers: Helping under-5s Live Active and Healthy Lives*. London: BHF.

Developmental Milestones, www.foundationyears.org.uk/your-babys-development/

Students and practitioners also need to be aware that the direction of physical development follows two patterns:

- from head to toe (cephalo-caudal) whereby head and neck control is acquired before control of the spinal muscles, then rolling, shuffling, crawling and walking;
- from inner to outer (proximo-distal), brain, spinal column before shoulders, arms and hands and lastly fine motor control of fingers.

(Neaum, 2013, p50)

Knowing this should help prevent the urge to move children through developmental sequences before they are ready; for example, expecting children to hold a pencil in a pincer grip to write before they have control of their shoulder, arm and hand. Some children may be 6 or 7 years old before they have the required level of control to write. Gross motor skills must be refined before fine motor skills will be fully developed.

Gross motor skills are generally understood as whole body movements, for example rolling, standing, walking and running and require, strength, stamina, balance, stability and agility. Fine motor skills refer to precise finger and hand movements which rely on hand–eye coordination, that is, the body's ability to coordinate the visual system with the motor system (adapted from BHF, 2013, p5).

It is essential that children are supported through developmentally appropriate play to develop both gross and fine motor skills. The UK physical activity guidelines for the under-5s (DoH, 2011) recommend that pre-school children who can walk unaided should be physically active for at least 180 minutes, spread throughout the day, and all under-5s should minimise the time being sedentary. Continuous provision indoors and outdoors that enables children to play spontaneously will provide them with exercise, fun and stimulation but supporting physical development means ensuring that the children acquire

- muscle strength and control;
- suppleness;
- balance;

- confidence;
- stamina.

In addition, students and practitioners should ensure when planning for physical development they consider the whole body, legs, arms and shoulders, backs, and equally the development of smaller muscles including hands and wrists, feet and ankles, and faces.

REFLECTION ACTIVITY 4.5

Consider a range of equipment available in most settings, including balls, parachutes, slides, wheeled vehicles, milk crates, planks, bean bags, tunnels, puzzles, gardening tools, construction materials and programmable equipment. How might you incorporate these into your planning to support the development of gross and fine motor skills?

Health and self-care

Young children also require a healthy balanced diet, rest and sleep in order to grow and develop physically. Children's safety is of overriding importance, so students and practitioners must ensure equipment is set up correctly, well maintained and includes sufficient challenge. For children with disabilities suitable adjustments need to be made; students and practitioners should work closely with parents to ensure their physical development needs can be met.

REFLECTION ACTIVITY 4.6

To ensure you have a good understanding of physical development in young children, take some time to research the developmental milestones and consider how young children develop physical literacy. Useful sources of information are:

Physical literacy:

Whitehead, M (2010) The concept of physical literacy, in Whitehead, M. (ed) *Physical Literacy throughout the Lifecourse*. Abingdon: Routledge, pp11–12.

Physical development milestones:

Sharma, A and Cockerill, H (2014) *Mary Sheridan's from Birth to Five Years: Children's Developmental Progress* (4th edn). London: Routledge.

COMMUNICATION AND LANGUAGE

Communication and language development was designated as a prime area of learning because of its significant influence on reducing inequalities in achievement outcomes between different groups of children. Research conducted by Hart and Risley (1995) found that a key factor in children's development of language skills was the amount of language that children heard during their early years. Children whose parents/main carers spoke to them more frequently and engaged them in conversations developed more vocabulary and were more likely to practise using language, gaining confidence and more highly developed communication and language skills. Hart and Risley established that low-income children are exposed to 30 million fewer words than their higher-income peers before the age of three. Thus, these children start school with significantly impoverished language in comparison to their peers, despite them all having started to speak at around the same age. Although the home environment is the most significant influence on children's communication and language development, these research findings also have implications for practitioners when planning for communication and language.

PLANNING FOR A LANGUAGE RICH ENVIRONMENT

The most crucial element in planning for communication and language is for practitioners to plan for a language rich environment.

✓ TIPS FOR PRACTICE

A language rich environment promotes interactions between children, and between adults and children, and planning should include routines, resources and physical spaces.

- Routines to consider are personal care routines, snack times, group gathering times, storytime and singing and the times allocated for children to initiate their own play, but with adults available to provide new vocabulary and model language structures.
- Resources that promote communication and language are any types of resources that appeal to children's current interests, since they will stimulate communication in its many forms as well as opportunities to practise and extend language. The use of books, puppets, digital technology, small world and role play are all also effective in motivating children to communicate in their preferred mode and to begin to use language.
- Physical spaces do need careful planning if they are to support communication and language. This could involve creating communication friendly spaces (Jarman, 2007) in which children can gather in small, cosy and quiet spaces to enjoy a book or explore a resource together or with a key person. Additionally, outdoor areas can also support communication, as they provide ample opportunities for children to listen and tune into different sounds as well as developing communication skills for planning, negotiating and questioning.

REFLECTION ACTIVITY 4.7

Consider your work or placement setting. Can you identify areas which provide a language rich environment?

Now look at the section in *Development Matters* (Early Education, 2012) that covers Communication and Language (pp 15–21) for the age group of children you work with. Read through the two columns, 'Positive Relationships' and 'Enabling Environments'. What could you plan to do or provide to increase the opportunities for children to develop their communication and language skills?

THREE ASPECTS OF COMMUNICATION AND LANGUAGE

There are three aspects to this prime area of learning:

- listening and attention;
- understanding;
- speaking.

Listening and attention

Babies engage in listening and giving attention from the moment they are born, and even whilst in the womb. They develop ability to engage in 'conversations' through eye contact, gazing, imitating mouth movements, vocalising and moving their whole body, and also communicate their wish to end a 'conversation' by looking away and ignoring the adult (McEvoy, 2019). These early interactions support the forming of strong attachments leading to positive self-esteem and self-awareness. They require physical control and exercise too. One of the main priorities, therefore, when planning for the development of communication and language, is the need to plan carefully for an environment that is conducive to supporting listening and attention. The guidance in *Development Matters* is concise in its advice to 'keep background noise to a minimum, e.g. use music or radio briefly only for particular purposes' (Early Education, 2012, p15). This is because it is difficult for babies and younger children to tune into sound and maintain attention when surrounded by background noises, including music. In addition to planning for the physical environment, practitioners may also plan specific times or experiences for children to focus their attention and develop their listening skills through social interactions and group times. There are many examples listed in the *Development Matters* guidance to support children to tune into the sounds around them or notice differences in noises. These include playing games, exploring musical instruments, listening to stories or simply exploring the everyday resources in their environment.

Understanding

This aspect of learning is often not planned for in advance, but is greatly promoted and supported through adults' responses to children, which may be described as 'in the moment' planning. An example of this type of planning would be where a practitioner is chatting with a child or playing alongside them. The child demonstrates their understanding through language or actions and the adult capitalises on this opportunity to affirm or extend the child's understanding. This may involve the adult repeating back what the child has said, or asking a question to support reflection and thinking. When adults speak out loud as they do things or say what they are thinking, it may support 'sustained shared thinking' (Sylva et al., 2004), a process in which the adult and child work together in an intellectual way, sharing what they are thinking in order to solve a problem or develop their understanding of a concept. The guidance in *Development Matters* reminds us that children's understanding is usually more advanced than their speaking skills, so it is important for the practitioner to observe children carefully to ascertain their level of understanding and to scaffold their development of speech through the use of visual prompts and physical actions. Most importantly, the role of the adult is crucial in providing the child with a breadth of vocabulary and planning for regular opportunities to hear language.

Speaking

Learning to speak is a complex process. It is intrinsically linked to personal, social and emotional development and physical development. Learning to speak requires children to have the confidence to have a go at speaking and to persevere when they are not understood. It requires adults to model how to articulate the speech sounds and to introduce new vocabulary for children to draw on. Therefore, when planning for this aspect of communication and language you should plan holistically across several areas of learning and plan multiple opportunities for children to be able to speak in different contexts. *Development Matters* (Early Education, 2012, pp19–21) lists suggestions on how to support children to develop their speech and advises that adults should allow children plenty of time to process their thoughts and plan their responses to questions or comments. For some children the development of speech may be delayed by a physical impairment or an emotional influence. For others, learning to speak English may be delayed if it is not their home language. Nevertheless, despite these specific needs, it is helpful to remember that for all children the use of alternative forms of communication such as visual prompts and signing are a necessary scaffold in developing their speech, language and communication skills.

REFLECTION ACTIVITY 4.8

Do you need to develop more knowledge about how children learn to speak? Which of the following suggestions would help you?

- further reading (see suggestions at the end of this chapter)
- seek professional development through a training course
- observe how more experienced or more qualified colleagues model language to children
- ask a colleague to observe you and provide critical feedback on how you communicate with and model language to children

CONCLUSION

The three prime areas of learning are the foundations for all areas of learning and development. They are interdependent and inextricably linked. Personal, social and emotional development requires you to plan for and commit to the key person approach. This is at the heart of effective planning for emotional development and should be reflected in policies and routines outlined in the setting's operational plan. Physical development involves planning for fine and gross motor skills as well as healthy lifestyles, including mental and physical health. This may be planned for through specific activities such as movement play sessions, or incorporated into continuous provision planning through outdoor play. Communication and language involves planning for a language rich environment and careful consideration of the teaching strategies to be used by practitioners, ensuring they are appropriately matched to the developmental needs of the children.

FURTHER READING

Archer, C and Siraj, I (2015) *Encouraging Physical Development Through Movement-Play*. London: Sage.

Langston, A (2014) *Facilitating Children's Learning in the EYFS*. Maidenhead: Open University Press.

Tassoni, P (2018) *Understanding Children's Behaviour: Learning to Be with Others in the Early Years*. London: Featherstone.

REFERENCES

Bowlby, J (1969) *Attachment and Loss. Vol 1: Attachment*. London: Hogarth.

Bowlby, J (1988) *A Secure Base: Clinical Applications of Attachment Theory*. London: Routledge.

British Heart Foundation (BHF) (2013) *Early Movers: Helping Under-5s Live Active and Healthy Lives*. London: British Heart Foundation.

Department for Education (DfE) (2017) *Statutory Framework for the Early Years Foundation Stage: Setting the Standards for Learning, Development and Care for Children from Birth to Five*. London: DfE.

Department of Health (DoH) (2011) *Start Active, Stay Active: A Report on Physical Activity for Health from the UK Chief Medical Officers*. London: Department of Health.

Early Education (2012) *Development Matters in the Early Years Foundation Stage (EYFS)*. London: Early Education. Available at https://www.foundationyears.org.uk/wp-content/uploads/2012/03/Development-Matters-FINAL-PRINT-AMENDED.pdf

Goodsir, K (2016) Holistic development: the physical development of children, in Trodd, L (ed) *The Early Years Handbook for Students and Practitioners*. London: Routledge, pp246–61.

Hart, B and Risley, T R (1995) *Meaningful Differences in the Everyday Experiences of Young American Children*. Baltimore, MD: Brookes Publishing.

Jarman, E (2007) *Communication Friendly Spaces: Improving Speaking and Listening Skills in the Early Years Foundation Stage*. Nottingham: Basic Skills Agency.

Langston, A (2014) *Facilitating Children's Learning in the EYFS*. Maidenhead: Open University Press.

McEvoy, J (2019) Communication and language, in McMahon, S and Dyer, M (eds) *Advanced Work-Based Practice in the Early Years: A Guide for Students*. London: Routledge, pp101–15.

Manning-Morton, J (2014) Young children's personal, social and emotional development: foundations of being, in Mukehrji, P and Dryden, L (eds) *Foundations of Early Childhood: Principles and Practice*. London: Sage.

Neaum, S (2013) *Child Development for Early Years Students and Practitioners*. London: Sage.

Sylva, K, Melhuish, E, Sammons, P, Siraj-Blatchford, I and Taggart, B (2004) *The Effective Provision of Pre-School Education (EPPE) Project*. London: DfES.

5 PLANNING FOR THE SPECIFIC AREAS OF LEARNING

Alison Ryan

CHAPTER AIMS

By the end of this chapter you will be able to:

*   understand the importance of the specific areas of learning – Literacy, Mathematics, Understanding the World, Expressive Arts and Design – and how they link together
*   make appropriate use of key ideas such as the importance of reading and the teaching of phonics in your work with children
*   appreciate the links between Literacy and Mathematics and the importance of language in mathematics learning
*   take account of holistic and child centred pedagogy when thinking about planning for children's learning in these areas

As you read this chapter, refer to pages 28–46 of *Development Matters in the Early Years Foundation Stage (EYFS)* (Early Education, 2012).

LITERACY

This specific area has two aspects:

*   reading;
*   writing.

Speaking and listening are not included because they are part of the prime area of communication and language. Although it may seem too early to talk about reading and writing with very young children, the foundations of success in these areas start from a very young age. Research such as the important work by Parsons and Bynner (1998, 2002) with adults born in 1958 and followed through a longitudinal study into adulthood, showed that children who struggled with literacy at the age of 7 were not likely to improve their skills on their own and subsequently were at risk of educational and social exclusion.

Since 1997 with the introduction of the National Literacy Strategy there has been a government focus on literacy within all areas of the curriculum, starting with Early Years, throughout formal schooling and also within adult education and family learning, acknowledging that there are many parents who need support with their own skills and who may need support to help their children. Building a good foundation for learning by developing a love of reading and writing is key for all Early Years practitioners. This work has been supported by organisations such as the National Literacy Trust (2018), who have useful research and publications on supporting literacy in settings and for parents.

Bouley (2013) has identified five predictors of early literacy: oral language, phonemic awareness, alphabet awareness, concepts about print, and early writing with inventive spelling. These areas are very important to develop so that when children do start their formal learning they have a good awareness of these concepts. This starts from birth when we talk and sing to new-born babies and carries on until children develop their own skills as confident readers and writers.

READING

When beginning to work on developing reading with very young children, practitioners will be supporting children with the receptive skills of reading rather than the productive skills. That is to say that younger children will be being read to rather than solely reading for themselves. It is vital to encourage children to access books from a very early age as, even though they will not be reading for themselves in the fullest sense, a love of being read to helps in a large number of ways. They also need to develop skills of accessing books such as knowing which way up to hold them, being able to turn the pages and appreciating the idea that you can read either to yourself or to an audience. Reading stories with children also helps develop awareness of narrative and sequencing, which is vital for later work in writing in Key Stage 1. This can be supported by practitioners asking questions such as, 'can you remember what happens next?' Repetition is key; children need to hear a word many times to be able to learn it and will not get bored by re-reading the same favourite story over and over again.

A key part of alphabet awareness and learning the concepts of print is recognising literacy within the environment. Even before children learn to read they can recognise what we term social signs such as labels on toilets and companies and services they are familiar with, for example the big yellow M of McDonald's or the petrol company logo at a service station. This is key to helping them understand that print conveys meaning and that the written word can be used to identify, inform, instruct and entertain. This can be linked to environmental literacy, where name labels and equipment labels with pictures help children to sort, match and tidy up, which also contributes to mathematical skills as well. As Neumann et al. state:

> *Thus, during toddlerhood this ability to differentiate between symbolic systems of pictures, letters and numbers, and to understand that they hold a communicative function, paves the way for early literacy development.*

(Neumann et al., 2011, p234)

REFLECTION ACTIVITY 5.1

Environmental literacy in your setting

Look at the displays that are in your setting. How do they contribute to the overall learning of literacy? Is children's work displayed and why? Is it aimed at the parents to show skill development or to celebrate children's achievement?

What about aspects of literacy such as labels? Do the children have name labels on their coat pegs, cups etc.? Are other things labelled such as storage for toys? Is any of this labelling supported by pictures?

There are many different debates about the best way to teach reading; however, since the Rose Review (Rose, 2006), systematic synthetic phonics has been the preferred method of teaching reading in the UK. The Department for Education published a supporting document for settings, *Letters and Sounds* (DfE, 2007), shortly after the review. While many settings now use commercial phonics packages such as Read Write Inc. or Jolly Phonics, this is still a very useful publication to read to make yourself aware of what phonemic awareness is about and how you can incorporate that into your practice. The document is divided into phases that support pre-reading and writing, starting with Phase One which covers awareness of sounds. There are no set age bands for using the phases with children; it is done as part of the everyday activities within the setting for all children that can access it.

✓   TIPS FOR PRACTICE

When reading with children you should be thinking about both of these aspects of sound such as oral blending and segmenting, basically how we make up words from different sounds and letter combinations. Thinking about blends such as sh, ch, th and where they occur in books and looking for opportunities to discuss sounds with children are vital to developing their phonemic awareness.

REFLECTION ACTIVITY 5.2

The books in your setting

Carry out an audit of the book stock in your setting. Are there books suitable for all ages, such as sturdier board books for younger children and without print for older children? Are the books easily accessible for the children and are they allowed free access to them? What are the favourite books, both for practitioners and children? Do the books in your setting reflect the diversity of UK culture? Are there different types of people and families represented?

WRITING

For very young children the most important thing is the development of gross and fine motor skills, including grasp and hand and arm strength, that will enable them to be able to write later on. Children go through four stages of grasp (SWNHS, 2018) between the ages of 1 year and around 6 years. This leads to the development of dynamic tripod grasp that enables them to hold a pen or pencil with two fingers and thumb with enough control for accurate letter formation. From around the age of 1 they will be starting to grasp mark-making tools in the palmar grasp, with the hand wrapped around the tool. Settings should have equipment suitable for early mark making, such as wider pens and crayons that are easier for small fingers to hold.

Pre-writing skills are not just about being able to hold a pen or pencil and it is important that children get lots of opportunity for sensory stimulation such as palm printing, and messy play with shaving foam, sand and playdough, which will all help in developing their fine motor skills and the development of their grasp. The DfE publication *Mark Making Matters* (2008) is another useful resource to look at for the development of children's drawing and writing skills and gives very useful guidance about how to make mark making accessible to all children.

It is also important that children become aware of the writing around them, as mentioned previously, and that they realise that writing has meaning and that this can be important in many different ways. One of the earliest things that children may discover is that the letters in their own name occur in other places, which can be very exciting for them.

When looking at how children develop their reading and writing skills it is useful to have an idea of the different stages that they go through. The Reading and Writing Scales developed by the Centre for Literacy in Primary Education (CLPE, 2016) are a very useful guide for practitioners.

✓ TIPS FOR PRACTICE

For children with English as an Additional Language (EAL), it is also important to recognise potential differences in the child's home language and English at several different levels. The language may differ in terms of the alphabet used, orientation of writing, for example starting on the left rather than the right-hand side of the page, and in the grammar rules used. Early mark making may show aspects of both languages if the children are being taught their home language by parents or carers, so practitioners should find out as much as possible about a child's language background in order to support literacy learning.

MATHEMATICS

Mathematics in the Early Years is divided into two aspects:

- numbers;
- shape, space and measure.

Most of this learning in mathematics is about the language of mathematics, developing understanding of words such as one, five, triangle, longer, weigh and share.

It is important to develop this language from birth. For babies, things like counting toes and fingers, rhymes such as 'Round and Round the Garden', 'Wheels on the Bus', and 'Five Little Speckled Frogs' help develop awareness of positional language, numbers and of the difference between cardinal numbers (one, two, three etc. that we use for counting) and ordinal numbers (first, second, third etc. that we use for ordering).

REFLECTION ACTIVITY 5.3

The language of mathematics

Select any piece of play equipment from your setting – it could be a toy or a piece of construction equipment. Think about all of the mathematics language that can link to it, e.g. size, shape, positional language, language of time, language describing speed etc.

Think about how you could use this language when interacting with a child playing with this equipment.

Butterworth (2005) discusses the important idea of numerosity which is linked to cardinal numbers. Numerosity is about knowing the number of things in a set and it is one of the first things that we teach children to do, to count how many there are. This can be integrated into practice in many different ways such as counting how many pieces of fruit are on a plate to counting how many children are in class that day.

There are many links between literacy and mathematics. Carruthers and Worthington (2005) developed the term 'mathematical graphics' to discuss the specific acts of mark making that children use when recording mathematics thinking. This covers both the use of numbers and other things such as tallying or recording in different ways; for example, a child may draw four circles on a page to represent four apples.

✓ TIPS FOR PRACTICE

It is important the children see adults modelling the recording of mathematics information such as prices, weights, heights etc. An example of doing this is having a height chart on the wall that children can use to measure themselves and marks can be made to show height over time. This can link in very well with discussion of age, e.g. are all 3-year-olds the same height? Is the tallest child also the oldest child? When do we stop growing?

UNDERSTANDING THE WORLD

Understanding the world has three aspects:

- people and communities;
- the world;
- technology.

The links between these and the first two specific areas, literacy and mathematics, can be used to widen children's experiences of their own lives and immediate environment. Much of what is identified as good practice links clearly with aspects of communication, reading and writing, in using books and film to bring other cultures and experiences into the setting.

It is important to recognise the diversity of UK culture and to have access to resources and role play areas that reflect this and to think about how you are using other forms of literacy. For example, on a walk to the shops with older children they could be encouraged to look for evidence of use of other alphabets for signs etc., and photos of these can be taken for display at the setting. If you do not have this in the locality, you could use pictures sourced from the internet of things such as an advert in Urdu or a restaurant sign in Chinese. This can be extended into the role play area by thinking about visiting different types of restaurants, trying different foods from other cultures or countries. Where possible, the experience should be as authentic as you can get; it is much more exciting to see noodles being cooked and to try the different types rather than have a play set of plastic Chinese food. Describing taste and texture all helps with language development.

✓ **TIPS FOR PRACTICE**

Links with mathematics can be made in other areas too. A visit to a farm park or zoo will enable children to relate the sizes of different animals that they have seen and this again can be supported by displays. A visit to a local park to look at all the different trees and shrubs can be used to display different shapes and colours of leaves and to think about seasonal changes, as time is part of the measurement area of mathematics.

Technology can be used effectively within literacy and mathematics; for example, pull back toys versus push toys can be used for discussions on different speeds, and older children can be encouraged to think about ways of measuring and recording these investigations. Digital cameras are a really good resource here as is digital video, which can also be used to capture role play and visits so that children can discuss what they were doing after the event. Within the area of measurement, comparing digital scales with non-digital gives a useful opportunity for mathematical literacy and links in to practical tasks such as baking.

EXPRESSIVE ARTS AND DESIGN

Expressive arts and design is made up of two aspects:

- exploring and using media and materials;
- being imaginative.

The use of media and materials has already been identified as vital for developing pre-writing skills. The use of all different sorts of paint, crayons, chalks etc. will also give children the opportunity for language development as well as the actual creation of visual pieces that can be used for discussion. Music is based on mathematical principles and a lot of what you will be exploring with the children are aspects such as beats, moving to music and thinking about music being fast or slow.

✓ TIPS FOR PRACTICE

In a practical way there are also lots of links between expressive arts and design and mathematics. The content of the mathematics curriculum contains work on shape and space that relates to the planning out of work and the use of shape to create art. A really good idea for older children is to look at some mathematically or geometrically inspired art such as the work of Mondrian, or to provide shapes for the children to use for their art. This area of work also brings in symmetry and ideas of proportion, looking at the different shapes of things in the environment. It also links to the ideas of pattern and repeating pattern which is a key underpinning for understanding things such as multiplication tables in later learning. Mixing paint is a good way to introduce ideas about simple ratio and proportion, for example, the more white paint we put into the black paint the paler it gets and by mixing equal parts of blue and red we can make purple.

HOLISTIC PLANNING WITHIN CONTINUOUS PROVISION

It is sometimes easier to make links between literacy and other subjects, as reading and writing are obviously involved in accessing and understanding information about all subjects. It may be harder to see the connections between mathematics and other areas. One of the key things about holistic planning is to look for the topics that can be integrated within an activity rather than try and force things artificially into the activity. It is about thinking in a different way and sometimes seeing things differently. For us as adults we have been used to thinking about mathematics as a separate curriculum area, taught in a very discrete way with few obvious links to other areas. For young children who have not yet experienced a formal secondary school curriculum that is not the case, however; as Robertson explains here:

> The world is a mathematical place. For young children who are naturally curious there are shapes, numbers, moving objects and patterns to behold, things to count and investigations to be undertaken. It is a creative, challenging and wondrous way of looking at life and exploring the world.

> (Robertson, 2017, p1)

When looking for creative ideas for child-led planning, think about where the children already experience number, shape and space. This leads you to be able to think about how each area of continuous provision can support mathematics and literacy rather than just having designated literacy and mathematics areas. It may be useful to conduct an observation of how children are using your continuous provision and see which areas are most used, then focus on providing more mathematics and literacy within those areas. One of the things to look out for is what Bryce-Clegg (2013, p34) calls 'stagnation', which is where children are going to the same areas of provision and using the same resources all the time so those well used areas need to be providing lots of different opportunities rather than just the same sand, water and small world play.

Within his book there is a really useful audit of all of the different types of provision, showing very clearly the mathematics and literacy in each area (Bryce-Clegg, 2013, pp41–9).

REFLECTION ACTIVITY 5.4

Consider the following example of an activity developed for water play by Early Years students at university.

The students filled the tray with strips of cellophane creating a really good sensory experience as it gave it the texture of seaweed. They then took some magnetic fish and attached numbers to them so children could have a go at catching the fish with rods.

Which aspects of physical development and mathematical development does this activity bring together?

When thinking about the skills that young children need to be able to access mathematics and literacy skills, much of it is sound awareness, both in terms of general sounds and what is termed auditory discrimination, being able to distinguish different sounds. A good example of this is where the Early Years students created a 'sound wall' in the music area where not only instruments but other noise making equipment is available for the children to access by being hung from strings on the back of a low shelving unit. These could be things like tambourines and shakers or general household items such as baking trays, whisks, metal and wooden spoons. The aim is to enable children to experience a range of different sounds and practitioners can work with children to get them to think about which is the loudest or softest sound, how the sounds are different, enabling them to key into different elements of sound which links in really well with the early phases of phonemic awareness.

Much of what we think of as play in other areas is mathematical play. Block or construction play, for example, is full of opportunities for looking at shapes, sorting and counting. Often it may be a case of restructuring the area to enable children to have full access to a wide range of material. One of the things to avoid is children feeling that they have to make certain things with the materials; at this age it is vital that they explore all of the materials available and work out their properties on their own. You may know that Duplo and wooden bricks are separate types of product but to a child working out what goes together and what doesn't is an essential part of developing problem solving skills, which are a key part of mathematics learning. It may be easier for tidying up if you only have one set of construction toys out at a time but it makes for a much richer learning environment if the children can experiment with lots of different materials in their play.

✓ TIPS FOR PRACTICE

It is also important to think about the outdoor spaces as part of the continuous provision that can be used to enhance mathematics and literacy as well as understanding the world rather than being seen as somewhere just to play with larger toys such as bikes. Keith (2017) writes about organising the outdoor area into learning spaces rather than just being seen as a play area and gives some good examples of how this provision can enhance learning. A planting area, for example, can enable children to dig which is very good for motor skills development and hand strength and the planting of seeds and caring for them brings in lots of aspects of basic science such as the plants' need for water and sunlight. Naming of the different types of things planted, verbally by the practitioner and children and by having plant labels, contributes to the outdoor environmental literacy, and harvesting any plants grown gives an opportunity for counting and comparison of size. One really good idea for this is growing sunflowers as they are very robust and grow to a good height, enabling young children to get experience of language such as taller and shorter.

A key aspect of developing pre-writing skills is the development of hand strength. This can be developed through lots of different aspects of manipulation. Using the instruments and sound making equipment mentioned above is one way of developing grip, as is construction play. As well as developing sensory awareness, playdough is a really good way of enabling children to develop hand strength. It takes a lot of manipulation to do things like roll out dough and press down with cutters. There are some good ideas as well in the kind of exercises used in 'dough disco', where music is used along with a specific series of actions to help children develop their hand and finger movements. More information on this can be found in the references list (Bason, 2018), and there are some good resources to use on YouTube.

To enable full access to reading in your provision, try to ensure that you have fiction and non-fiction books in every area, not just in a reading corner. Ensure these are changed regularly to support other themes such as seasonal or activity planning. This will mean that children have access to books at all times, not just those children who like going to the reading corner, and this can enable you as the practitioner to model how you might use a book to find out information or to tell stories about a topic.

REFLECTION ACTIVITY 5.5

Audit of fiction and non-fiction books

Carry out an audit of fiction and non-fiction books at your setting to see how they would fit in to all areas of provision. How are fiction and non-fiction books identified and are books on display throughout the setting or just in one place?

A good example of this holistic planning was in an area set up by Early Years students in what was the role play area of the classroom setting. They themed the area as a baby clinic, incorporating fiction and non-fiction books on visiting the doctor and using props such as weighing scales and feeding bottles with millilitres on to support mathematical learning. There were posters displayed and simplified forms for the children to complete to support literacy development in recording the name of the baby being examined, their weight and any other details. This not only would support the children in their mathematics and literacy development but also link with understanding the world, as most children will have experienced visiting either the doctor or a specific baby clinic with younger siblings thus allowing them to explore that experience within the setting. The same sorts of ideas can be used for a vets' surgery or a florist where children can be involved in making and pricing the stock as well as taking orders verbally or by filling in forms.

Holistic planning needs us to think about the child as the starting point and to follow their interests rather than thinking about lots of different areas of development. Observing a child and looking at what they want to do is the starting point and then thinking about how you can incorporate other areas into their preferences. Children do not see the world as divided into different areas of learning with outcomes for each one, rather they see it as somewhere that can offer endless possibilities for exploration and enjoyment and so, to be really effective, as Early Years practitioners we need to always be in touch with that inner 2-, 3- or 4-year-old.

FURTHER READING

Briggs, M (2015) *Creative Teaching: Mathematics in the Early Years and Primary Classroom* (2nd edn). Abingdon: Routledge.

Johnson, J and Watts, A (2018) *Developing Creativity and Curiosity Outdoors: How to Extend Creative Learning in the Early Years*. Abingdon: Routledge.

Tucker, K (2014) *Mathematics through Play in the Early Years* (3rd edn). London: Sage.

Whitebread, D and Coltman, P (2015) *Teaching and Learning in the Early Years* (4th edn). Abingdon: Routledge.

REFERENCES

Bason, S (2018) Let's go to the dough disco. Available at www.spreadthehappiness.co.uk/product/dough-disco-book/

Bouley, T (2013) Five predictors of early literacy. Available at www.youtube.com/watch?v=HqImgAd3vyg

Bryce-Clegg, A (2013) *Continuous Provision in the Early Years*. London: Bloomsbury.

Butterworth, B (2005) The development of arithmetical abilities. *Journal of Child Psychology and Psychiatry*, 46(1): 3–18.

Carruthers, E and Worthington, M (2006) *Children's Mathematics: Making Marks, Making Meaning* (2nd edn). London: SAGE.

Centre for Literacy in Primary Education (CLPE) (2016) Available at https://clpe.org.uk/library-and-resources/reading-and-writing-scales

Department for Education (2007) *Letters and Sounds*. Available at www.gov.uk/government/publications/letters-and-sounds

Department for Education (2008) *Mark Making Matters*. Available at www.foundationyears.org.uk/wp-content/uploads/2011/10/Mark_Marking_Matters.pdf

Early Education (2012) *Development Matters in the Early Years Foundation Stage (EYFS)*. London: Early Education. Available at https://www.foundationyears.org.uk/wp-content/uploads/2012/03/Development-Matters-FINAL-PRINT-AMENDED.pdf

Keith, L (2017) *Developing Young Children's Mathematical Learning Outdoors: Linking Pedagogy and Practice*. Abingdon: Routledge.

National Literacy Trust. Available at https://literacytrust.org.uk/

Neumann, M M, Hood, M, Ford, R M and Neumann, D L (2012) The role of environmental print in emergent literacy. *Journal of Early Childhood Literacy*, 12(3): 231–58.

Parsons, S and Bynner, J (1998) *Influences on Adult Basic Skills: Factors Affecting the Development of Literacy and Numeracy from Birth to 37*. London: Basic Skills Agency.

Parsons, S and Bynner, J (2002) *Basic Skills and Social Exclusion: Findings from a Study of Adults Born in 1970*. London: Basic Skills Agency.

Robertson, J (2017) *Messy Maths: A Playful, Outdoor Approach for Early Years*. Carmarthen, Wales: Independent Thinking Press.

Rose, J (2006) *Independent Review of the Teaching of Early Reading*. Available at http://dera.ioe.ac.uk/5551/2/report.pdf

SWNHS (2028) *Handwriting Development*. Available at www.swft.nhs.uk/application/files/5614/5995/2571/handwriting_development.pdf

6 PLANNING THE LEARNING ENVIRONMENT

Karen Smith and Mary Dyer

CHAPTER AIMS

By the end of this chapter you will be able to:

- understand the value of planning an environment for supporting learning
- understand the relationships between an enabling environment and a learning environment
- reflect on and evaluate your own practice in planning your learning environment

INTRODUCTION

The introduction of the Early Years Foundation Stage (EYFS) in 2008 acknowledged the importance of the environment in enabling young children to learn, identifying the value of a well-planned environment as a key principle that underpins good practice in Early Years settings (DCSF, 2008). Since then, in the revisions to statutory requirements and good practice that have followed (DfE, 2017; Early Education, 2012), the Early Years environment has retained its place as a key element in ensuring children reach a good level of development prior to starting their compulsory schooling. Its importance lies in what it provides for the children themselves, and how it can also support practitioners in implementing a high-quality, child-centred, play-based pedagogy. This chapter explains how the enabling environment of the current EYFS (DfE, 2017) represents a positive learning environment for children, and the role of the practitioner in developing and using this to meet their individual needs.

WHAT IS AN ENABLING ENVIRONMENT?

An enabling learning environment is described by Johnston (2013) as one that offers opportunity for children to explore the world around them as they interact with their peers and adults. For this reason, it is particularly important that the learning environment ignites children's curiosity and enthusiasm for learning and in turn children are enabled to form friendships and thrive (DfE, 2017). The guiding principles of the current EYFS recognise that children are unique, with individual learning needs, and different backgrounds and experiences that impact on them in different ways (DfE, 2017). They learn best from the foundation of positive relationships, and when they can explore independently, interact socially with adults and their peers, and when they are offered opportunities to encounter new and appropriately challenging experiences. Johnston (2013) highlights the promotion of individuality, support through transitions, and co-ordinated interagency working and parent/carer partnerships as central to the development of an enabling environment, as one in which learning may most effectively occur.

WHAT DOES A LEARNING ENVIRONMENT REQUIRE?

At a very practical level within a learning environment, practitioners need to know their children and their individual needs, to be able to offer a range of experiences and resources to support learning, and to set up activities and opportunities for interaction and relationship formation that will enhance children's development. However, the learning environment is also about children's sense of well-being and their emotional security and development. The EYFS requires practitioners to promote children's well-being as an essential underpinning for their learning, by offering children a sense of belonging in their setting, and the opportunity to be themselves and express their individuality (Wardle and Vesty, 2015). Ang (2014), drawing on work by Carr (2001), Carr and Claxton (2002) and Laevers (2000), argued that good social and emotional development supports the development of positive learning dispositions and a high level of engagement with their learning in young children, characteristics of learning which will support their progress in later schooling. The key person system (DfE, 2017), discussed later in this chapter, forms an essential part of this social and emotional support and therefore is vital to fostering an effective learning environment.

The enabling environment is also considered to include the child's wider community – their culture, their family, their social networks, the community services they encounter – as well as the different agencies and support services they use. An effective learning environment is one in which individual children's cultures and family backgrounds are valued to promote a sense of belonging and self-esteem, and where services work together to support a child's learning.

This chapter now considers how practitioners can develop an enabling and effective learning environment, beginning with how they can use the environment to establish a welcome and a sense of belonging and well-being in children. It then discusses how the physical environment can be set up to promote learning, before going on to discuss how you might use research and theory to inform your planning of a learning environment, and how, in planning *your* learning environment, you can respect and take account of the voice of the child. It will conclude by discussing the importance of reflection in planning your learning environment, and exploring how this can include the perspectives of all those who might be considered to be stakeholders in this process.

AN OUTSIDE-IN APPROACH

The learning environment, as the term suggests, is about 'the environment' in which learning takes place. Once we begin to consider this in detail, many more elements of what we actually mean by the learning environment are to be considered. To understand what this means, let us take an 'outside-in' approach. This approach takes the view that a well-planned learning environment begins outside the building and follows through to the inside. The EYFS statutory guidance (DfE, 2017) highlights the importance of practitioners preparing a secure foundation through learning and development opportunities, but it is a forward thinking and creative practitioner who will consider this principle to include not only the infrastructure of the play spaces inside the learning environment, but also the approach to the setting too. As children, parents and carers approach the setting, it can be argued that their learning starts at that point. Children need to familiarise themselves with the outside aesthetics of their learning environment before even stepping foot inside. If, on approach, the learning environment is not attractive and welcoming, then children are not going to feel as inspired to enter as those who have an 'outside-in' approach that is embracing and stimulating. So what can be done to ensure we enthuse our children and parents from the very point of entering the setting's outside area?

✓   TIPS FOR PRACTICE

Taking an outside-in approach, welcoming signposting is essential and in some settings this has been done both pictorially and in the written form. A clear route that leads the children to the entrance helps them to feel they are welcomed. This means that access points should be clear of clutter and, where possible, include a dash of colour. A child friendly 'welcome' sign is helpful, and for parents, somewhere to station prams and buggies.

Children learn and develop well in enabling environments, strengthened by a strong partnership between practitioners and parents (DfE, 2017) so it is of high importance that we take these steps to help families feel a sense of belonging. All these factors are small matters within themselves but put together they create an introduction to a learning environment that says, 'Hello, you are welcome'.

Once through the door, the welcoming theme needs to continue and this is where you can significantly add your creative flair. It is at this point that a child's emotional and social well-being becomes of high importance, based on the understanding that a child needs to feel secure in their knowledge that the practitioners around them really do care. Children are very intuitive, quickly recognising the attentiveness of adults, observed through not just what is said to them, but through our body language signals too. On entering the building, children usually have a designated space in which to hang coats and leave additional footwear and bags. Practitioners need to consider how this area draws the children over the threshold of their learning space that will inevitably become their play and learning area for the next 2–3 hours as a sessional arrangement or 6–7 hours if registered for the full day. Many cloakroom areas observed are colourful, pictorial and beautifully organised. This matters, not only for ease of access, but also for the reasons of unspoken messages these attributes convey. An organised, neatly set out cloakroom provides an essence of order to a child and communicates an expression of greeting. These factors are so important when encouraging and enthusing a child to join a learning environment, which, for some, can initially be daunting and intimidating.

REFLECTION ACTIVITY 6.1

Conduct an audit of your setting from the front door to the main rooms the children use, asking yourself:

- What is the first thing parents/carers and children see when they approach your setting?
- How welcoming and attractive is your entrance – does it tell newcomers who you are and what they can expect in your setting?
- Have you made organised space for the children's belongings?
- Are you making effective use of wall-space for displays and information?

Now think about what you might do to improve the approach to your setting.

THE EMOTIONAL ENVIRONMENT: KEY PERSON WORKING

Once through the doors and into the principal learning environment, the 'outside-in' approach should be truly realised. The essence of a vibrant learning environment not only relies on the fabric of the building and the resources within it but, crucially, the people within it as well. Each child's key person strives to meet their holistic needs but, crucially, this role also emphasises how the key person supports the emotional developmental characteristics of the child, forming a secure and stable foundation for learning with a sense of common well-being for all. Bowlby's attachment theory (1953) cited in Bruce (2011) demonstrates how children need the security of key people in their lives to enable them to emotionally flourish. It is a requirement of the EYFS statutory framework (DfE, 2017), based on this theory, that every registered Early Years provision has a key person system (Bruce, 2011), and every child is assigned a key person.

Unquestionably, as a key person, you have the privilege of developing strong emotional relationships with individual children and, in return for the trust that each child invests in you, you have a responsibility to ensure their learning experience is unique for each of them. Such responsibility may seem daunting, as though there is a huge weight of obligation and accountability on your shoulders, but this does not have to be the case. Instead you should feel a great sense of freedom to explore lots of ideas borne from children's conversation, actions and interests, and in return realise how the significance of your involvement supports their emotional well-being. Each key person knows their key children best and, therefore, through close and ongoing observation, assessment and planning, the milestones each child aspires to should be naturally realised rather than an enforced, obligatory requirement of the job. This way, children's individual needs and interests can be identified easily and quickly and then used to inform the planning of learning activities and experiences, in the knowledge that children have the security of established and emotionally balanced relationships needed to engage with their new environment. Parents and carers are equally supported by knowing there is a key person in the setting with detailed knowledge of their child, and with whom they can share information about the child's experiences and developments beyond the setting. Liaison between practitioner and parent/carer adds an additional layer of emotional enrichment to the child's overall experience within the setting.

THE PHYSICAL ENVIRONMENT

Wall displays are a valuable resource in terms of captivating a child's imagination and creativity and, of course, a strong sense of belonging. Wall displays, therefore, must be carefully planned to inspire and enhance the richness of a child's learning potential and it is through the use of displays that children are motivated to internalise positive images, new information and symbolisation of new knowledge and understanding. Practitioners need to be mindful that these factors must enhance the quality of learning experiences for all children and not just the majority. Depending on the demography of the setting, there will be groups of children whose individual needs require more focussed and individualised attention to ensure that their learning environment is equally enabling. This requires a deep sense of commitment and promise from practitioners. Without dedicated understanding of each child's specific needs, potentially some children may not be adequately supported through defined display work that reflects their culture, community and personal identity. Children who have English as an additional language and children who have special educational needs can sometimes experience missed opportunities to fully engage in their learning environment because practitioners have not unveiled their exact requirements. For this reason, it is imperative that displays are presented to the highest professional standards, making sure that wherever possible it is the children's own work that conveys the communicative messages and interpretations of their learning.

The practicalities of presenting professional, yet child-centred wall displays are focussed on colour, print, structure and order. The same principle applies to the physical layout of the play and learning spaces available to young children. Most settings have indoor and also outdoor space available to them, but let us think of these two spaces as two rooms, one indoor and the other outdoor. It is important that we see the outdoor space as another room rather than an area to be used when practitioners see fit, so that we develop the mind-set that the outdoors offers an equal amount of inspiration and stimulation as the carefully planned indoor space.

Research undertaken by the European Centre for Environment and Human Health (ECEHH) identified that when playing outside children prefer natural outdoor environments as opposed to man-made play spaces, which sadly have been found to decrease self-control and the capabilities of children (Frampton et al., 2015). This finding clearly highlights to the practitioner the relevance of high-quality outdoor provision that equally emulates the high-quality indoor provision to achieve an increase of children's self-control and capabilities. There is nothing more natural than to see children splashing in puddles, making mud pies and creating their own shelter using branches and foliage. Imagine how these outdoor experiences could be emulated within the inside room evoked by forward thinking, passionate and caring professionals!

Children enjoy zoned areas where they can experience more intimate learning opportunities as well as wider, more palatial areas for them to develop proficiency in gross motor competencies. The outdoor room therefore needs to have a quiet space, just in the same way we have a carpeted area with cushions inside. Similarly, the indoor room needs to have space for children to exert their physical energy; for example, using construction blocks which they not only build with, but can use to exercise their gross motor skills to balance, stride and crawl, in just the same way children do outside. These examples, along with many other opportunities to mirror the two rooms, can be achieved with careful planning that is determined by the needs of the children within the setting.

REFLECTION ACTIVITY 6.2

Design activities that complement each other between the indoor and outdoor spaces. How creative can you be when planning both indoor and outdoor rooms?

- Create an outdoor water play activity. Try to be creative, rather than simply duplicating the typical water tray. How can you ensure water play activities are accessible all year round?
- Create a role-play area outdoors. Find out what children want to see in it. Through sustained shared thinking you will find children will have many more ideas than you have.
- How can you create gross motor activities indoors that symbolise large equipment outdoors? Think about the best use of space as part of your planning for continuous provision.

As we consider both the indoors and outdoors as equal parts, then what goes into them should also be equally considered. In doing so, you will achieve an enabling environment, described by Johnston (2013) as a setting that brings together two key components: a supportive physical space, along with the warmth and attention created by the people within it. Within the two rooms, practitioners need to listen to and embrace the interests of each child in a positive way (Glazzard et al., 2010), ensuring their emotional and social development is enhanced by a unique and rich learning environment that encourages children to explore the world around them (Johnston, 2013). As we consider the viewpoints of Glazzard et al. (2010) and Johnston (2013), we can see that their perspectives on the learning environment capture three key components that together provide us with understanding that the genuine engagement of the practitioner within an enriched learning environment will in turn develop a playful learning experience that is created from a child's unique individuality. This vision is the basis on which to build an enabling environment that respects the cultures, communities and additional needs of the children and families of the setting. How amazing, therefore, is a learning environment that offers children play and learning opportunities that are mirrored between the two rooms? That the outdoor 'den' is substituted for a similar enclosed space within the indoor provision, and the mark-making table inside is mirrored as a large brush and paint activity in the outside room?

If we are to genuinely plan for the highest quality provision for children in our care, then we must take time to understand the true value of continuous provision. Bryce-Clegg (2013) identifies the risk that children's play resources can become a range of activities that simply keep the children occupied, rather than a well-considered range of activities that are meaningful and purposeful for enhancing learning. Models of play that focus on the child being central to their learning experience help us to understand how we should implement effective planning for the indoor and outdoor learning environments. Bruce's (2011) 12 features of play, which include playing alone, using representation and symbolic props and having their personal agenda, which may or may not be shared, can be a useful guide when planning play opportunities. Complementing this, Smith and Call's BASICS model (cited in Beckley, 2013) gives greater focus on a low stress environment and the child's inner emotions and dispositions, helping the practitioner to understand that quality provision starts with a sense of **b**elonging, **a**spiration, **s**afety and **i**ndividuality along with **c**hallenge and **s**uccess. Combining the two models helps us take a holistic perspective of the child when planning a quality Early Years environment.

USING RESEARCH AND THEORY TO PLAN THE LEARNING ENVIRONMENT

Practitioners' personal values and beliefs, and their knowledge and understanding of how young children learn, have a significant impact on how the learning environment is planned. Warden (2016) argues that practitioners can either consider themselves as directors of learning, focusing on an adult-led approach, or facilitators of learning, favouring a more child-centred approach to practice. Both approaches are considered necessary in terms of children's learning, and the approach a practitioner takes often follows the way in which they were taught. Many practitioners naturally strive to be a facilitator of learning, embedding the ethos of collaboration into the child's learning environment. But to become a facilitator you need to have faith in the child's direction (Bottrill, 2018). By using the teachings of educationalists that have gone before us, we can confidently underpin our practice with a broader understanding about why we do what we do.

This section offers some examples of how both historical and more recent research has contributed to current Early Years practice. Friedrich Froebel, working in the late eighteenth and early nineteenth centuries, recognised the value of natural resources and developed the term 'kindergarten' we use today. His focus on play and outdoor environments, coupled with adult guidance and support, offered children an environment for learning that was very different from the traditional classrooms associated with formal and compulsory education, and emphasised the value of nature as a learning resource. The Forest School provision of today reflects this value, and offers children learning opportunities with less adult structure and greater freedom to explore their natural world. Froebel's understanding of early childhood has clearly left an indelible mark on Early Years practitioners, reflected in the way we still refer to his work when planning pedagogical approaches. As we develop and grow our understanding of theoretical perspectives, we begin to realise that some of the research of today is built on the solid foundations of educationalists such as Froebel.

Research undertaken in Norway by Giske et al. (2018) considers the correlation between movement skills, play, social-emotional competence and well-being. Its findings show that without ability to move freely children will not develop relationships, self-confidence and self-awareness to appropriately manage their feelings and behaviour (Early Education, 2012). A corresponding research study carried out by Shoval et al. (2018) investigates mindful movement as an attribute towards higher level learning and reveals that young children who participate in learning activities that require a higher intensity of physical activity gain higher levels of cognitive development.

Interestingly, a comparative research study by Ellis et al. (2018) shows that, while practitioners may have every intention to provide dynamic continuous provision that offers lots of opportunity for movement and socialisation, it has been found that pre-school children on average tend to be sedentary for around 50 per cent of their time within a play and learning environment. Non-movement activities such as table-top games, circle time, story time and meal times, but also mark making, reading corners and painting do not in themselves ensure social learning will take place, whereas gross motor movement activities are more likely to do so. Alarmingly, practitioner participants of the study had thought that the children in their care were constantly active, by means of moving from one activity to another throughout the day. They had not realised just how much time children were spending as sedentary learners.

We need to consider, therefore, whether this revelation potentially jeopardises the research findings that show a correlation between movement and the development of children's social and emotional skills. If movement enhances social learning, then how do we ensure that the learning environment embeds this philosophy? However, you may argue that in fact children's activities that require little or no movement can still enhance social learning, but it is your responsibility to provide the rationale and justification for your decisions. This dichotomy is one of many that highlight the constant challenges Early Years practitioners face in finding the best ways to undisputedly ensure they are creating the best possible learning experience that validates the trueness of what we know young children should have. These examples of current research show that Froebel's philosophical understanding of children's needs to move around and explore, and his commitment to applying this to practice is just as important today, if not more so, and that we as practitioners are provided with a basis on which to build and reinforce knowledge and understanding about the key principles of planning an Early Years environment.

✓ TIPS FOR PRACTICE

To understand how different approaches to using the environment can support children's learning and development, visit different settings. If possible, visit a setting where children regularly participate in a Forest School. Observe the adults. Consider changing one thing in your outdoor provision; for example, make water more interesting by adding guttering to building blocks to help water flow and encourage children and practitioners to transport stones, cones and shells to the sand, water and mud.

Other educationalists, such as Montessori, Steiner and MacMillan should also be recognised as key advocates for children's learning, but it is important to note that each one has their own philosophy.

Maria Montessori applied the principles of Piaget's theories of how young children learn to the structure of her learning environments and to her practice, encouraging children to work at their own pace, through a series of stages, to understand particular concepts and processes. The MacMillan sisters set up nurseries with a combination of outdoor and indoor environments to support young children in understanding their world and worked with parents to improve their understanding of their children's developmental needs. Steiner believed that children should have the freedom to choose and explore with limited adult direction, creating an uninterrupted holistic learning experience. He believed in a flexible curriculum that resulted in resourceful children who were emotionally and intellectually equipped for a fast-changing world.

As practitioners, we need to decide which theorists or pioneers offer the best explanation of how young children learn, and then apply this to your planning of a learning environment. Loris Malaguzzi, founder of the world-renowned Reggio Emilia Early Years provision, stated, as one of his key principles of a purposeful and meaningful learning environment, that educators are researchers (Dubiel, 2016). With this in mind, you need to consider the balance of adult-led and child-led activity you use, how you will set out the space you have, how you will ensure access to an outdoor as well as an indoor space if you have both on offer, and how you will involve the children in your planning.

All these decisions should be based on theory, research and interpretation. A fully informed and active researcher practitioner will undoubtedly be a stronger advocate for learning in the Early Years but also one who is less likely to fall into the traps of bias and tunnel vision as we endeavour to create the best possible experience for the children in our care.

REFLECTION ACTIVITY 6.3

Having read this section about theory and research you will see how the work of Froebel has been interpreted in current research enquiry relevant to today's young children.

- Source current literature that reflects the work of a range of educationalists.
- Consider which theorists you recognise as influential to your practice, ideas and values.

THE VOICE OF THE CHILD

The Reggio Emilia philosophy of Early Years practice (Abbott and Nutbrown, 2005) and the Montessori approach (Garhart Mooney, 2000) regard the environment as a child's third teacher, after themselves and the adults around them, but also regard children as capable and competent learners rather than innocent but unknowing individuals who must rely totally on adults for their knowledge of the world. Similarly, Dahlberg and Moss (2005) argue that practitioners should adopt a 'pedagogy of listening' in their practice, giving children the space to construct their own understanding, both practically and intellectually, of their world. Through the Effective Provision of Pre-School Education (EPPE) project, Sylva et al. (2004) identify the importance of children's sustained shared thinking which requires time and opportunity to solely focus on what the child is saying, creating uninterrupted space to discuss, share ideas and *listen* to what is being said, placing a true and genuine value on the thoughts and feelings of the child. As practitioners, we can be guilty of being 'too busy' for many of these interactions to take place, but if you consider the enormous value and benefits derived from this type of collaboration you will come to realise that these interactions are just as important, even more so in some instances, than large group story time, large group circle time and other similar aspects of a typical day in pre-school provision. The concept of listening is something we can take for granted and something we do not always do very well. Bottrill (2018) discusses at length the importance of listening to children and explains that as practitioners we are so often busy in our adult world that we stifle the true meaning of the child's world. We become enveloped in organisational procedures, systems, policies and timetables to take us through the day and, while we most certainly need to adhere to these, we forget the essence of the voice of the child. Bottrill (2018) is concerned about the ways in which we inadvertently drown the child's voice by way of practising in an adult world, rather than practising 'in the moment', embracing the joyful and uncluttered thoughts of children.

Therefore, although it is the responsibility of the practitioner to plan an appropriate environment for learning, ensuring it is enabling for all children means taking into account their needs and preferences. We need to accommodate both adult led and child led activities, but crucially the key principle of planning is based on the joining of minds between the adults and children. It is important that when developing these connections to plan the learning environment, children also develop a sense of ownership and belonging too. Abbott and Nutbrown's (2005) reflections of their experiences of Reggio Emilia provision, which values individual children as competent, capable learners, discuss the strong bonds between practitioners and children, and indeed parents too. Practitioners, exercising their role as a key person, need to converge their adult viewpoints in terms of the planning requirements for the setting with the children's viewpoints, thus creating opportunity for sustained shared thinking (Sylva et al., 2004). The value of adults and children conferring in this way not only develops high level intellectual skills for the children involved, but also ensures that the learning environment planned reflects the children's wants and needs.

The United Nations Convention on the Rights of the Child (UNCRC) (UNICEF, 1989) recognises the rights of children both to play and learn, and to be consulted when decisions about their lives are made. By encouraging and valuing the input of children into our planning, we are encouraging in them a sense of well-being, and self-esteem, and fostering the positive dispositions to learning that will support them in later life. We are encouraging cooperation, collaboration and communication, and we are acknowledging them as individuals with a voice to be heard. We are also tapping into a rich vein of creativity, imagination and initiative, while encouraging the development of their problem-solving skills, their spatial awareness, and their fine and gross motor skills. Involving children in the planning of the learning environment is a learning experience for them and most importantly us. Children guide and steer us in the directions of learning they wish to take and therefore it is crucial that we take time to listen and act upon their choices. This reaps enormous benefits in the development of a positive social and emotional learning environment.

REFLECTION ACTIVITY 6.4

Consider your own practice and how often you involve children in the planning of your environment:

- How much choice and autonomy are they given?
- Are there resources that are not allowed outside – why? How can you overcome this?
- Could you involve the children more?
- Is there something that prevents you from getting children involved? What might they learn from being involved?

REFLECTING ON YOUR LEARNING ENVIRONMENT

Constant and timely reflective practice, evaluating the effectiveness of the planned learning environment will ensure that the continuous provision is exciting and vibrant, and that adult-led activities and routines continue to meet the individual needs of the children. Developing your own audit tools to review specific areas or aspects of provision (such as the one suggested earlier in this chapter) can be helpful in formalising your reflection and giving you a focus for discussion in team meetings. They are also a good way of involving other 'stakeholders' in reviewing your provision, such as parents/carers and also the children themselves, although you will need to think carefully about how you make these audits accessible and user-friendly for different groups of people. Using an established model for reflective thinking can be helpful, and a number of different models exist to structure reflective evaluation which can encourage you to link your actions to theory (Dyer and Firth, 2018; Jasper, 2013). It is useful to read up on several different approaches to find one that suits your style of thinking best.

To combine the perspectives of the different groups of people using your setting (children, their families, your colleagues) and to link your planning and practice to theory, Brookfield's Lenses (Brookfield, 2002) would seem to be an appropriate place to start. This model requires that, as you reflect, in this case on how you have planned your learning environment, you specifically consider what different people have told you, and also consider what research and theory have to say about an effective learning environment. This does not mean you need to consider the full range of theoretical perspectives, but you should revisit the pioneers of practice and the theorists whose work you consider to be most valid, and apply this to an evaluation of your own practice. You might find it helpful to produce a written account of your reflection, using a series of headings and sub-headings such as shown in Table 6.1.

Table 6.1   Example reflective report

REFLECTIVE REPORT

- **Planning/practice to be reviewed:** provide a brief description of the aspect of planning or area of the setting you are evaluating – a photograph or diagram, for example of a room layout, may be helpful here.
- **My own perspective:** what do you consider to be its strengths and weaknesses – be honest and objective, but avoid being over-critical or unrealistic in your evaluation; try to find evidence or reasons to support your ideas.
- **What do the children/the families/my colleagues think?** get some feedback from the appropriate people about this aspect of planning or area of the setting; just remember that you only need to include those groups most affected by this practice or aspect of planning, you do not always have to include everybody! User-friendly feedback sheets, wish lists and collegial team meetings are effective ways of drawing together feedback that might be helpful to you.
- **What does theory tell me?** do some research and apply this to current practice to evaluate how well you are using your background knowledge.
- **Action plan:** draw together all your information from these different perspectives and develop a realistic action plan for how you will make changes to your planning or use of the learning environment.

Be ready to evaluate again, once you have made the changes, to ensure that your practice is developing positively – reflection is a cycle rather than a simple linear process!

By using reflection in this way, you not only respect the needs and wishes of the children and families using your setting but you also draw upon your knowledge and understanding of the research and theory that underpins practice. Into this, you can also add the policies and guidelines that govern Early Years practice, so that you can be sure that your practice meets regulatory requirements and satisfactory standards, as well as taking account of current priorities and issues within Early Years education.

CONCLUSION

This chapter highlights many features of a high-quality learning environment, mindful of the underpinning principles of the EYFS statutory framework (DfE, 2017). In recognition of how children's social and emotional development is secured within a stimulating and resourceful learning environment, many strategies for planning have been discussed. Our outside-in approach emphasises the physical environment, whereas the value of a key person system captures the importance of intuitive and compassionate responses to children in support of their emotional stability and security. A clear and well-defined interpretation of an enabling environment is conveyed by highlighting ways in which the indoor and outdoor spaces become one with an uninterrupted free flow arrangement that demonstrates how continuous provision becomes accessible and supportive in meeting the individual needs of all children. Theoretical perspectives and contemporary research have been blended to demonstrate how we can make informed decisions when planning the learning environment, but also awakening us to the many challenges we face to achieve our desired outcomes.

One of these challenges is the imperative to hear and respect the voice of the child. This chapter strives to instil the concept that the child's voice is the sustenance for productive, lively and animated learning without which we are more likely to develop an undesirable, linear approach to practice, withholding from children their right to express an opinion, and to have that opinion taken into account (UNICEF, 1989). The voice of the child, central to their status as constructive learners (Dahlberg and Moss, 2005), sustains an ethos of transparency in our planning, embracing a sound and collective commitment by practitioners to provide the highest possible provision. The chapter concludes by considering how reflective evaluation of practice and planning can support this valuable ethos.

FURTHER READING

Bottrill, G (2018) *Can I Go and Play Now? Rethinking the Early Years.* London: Sage.
Dyer, M and Firth, N (2018) Being a reflective practitioner. In McMahon, S and Dyer, M (eds) *Work-based Practice in the Early Years: A Guide for Students.* Abingdon: Routledge.
Ellis, Y G, Cliff, D P and Okely, A D (2018) Childcare educators' perceptions of and solutions to reducing sitting time in young children: A qualitative study. *Early Childhood Education Journal,* 46: 377.

REFERENCES

Abbott, L and Nutbrown, C (2005) *Experiencing Reggio Emilia.* Maidenhead: Open University Press.
Ang, L (2014) Pre-school or prep school? Rethinking the role of Early Years education. *Contemporary Issues in Early Childhood,* 15(2): 185–99.

Beckley, P (ed) (2013) *The New Early Years Foundation Stage: Changes, Challenges and Reflections*. Maidenhead: Open University Press.

Bottrill, G (2018) *Can I Go and Play Now? Rethinking the Early Years*. London: Sage.

Bowlby, J (1953) *Child Care and the Growth of Love*. London: Penguin.

Brookfield, S D (2002) Using the lenses of critically reflective teaching in the community college classroom. *New Directions for Community Colleges, 118*: 31–8.

Bruce, T (2011) *Learning through Play: For Babies, Toddlers and Young Children* (2nd edn). London: Hodder Education.

Bryce-Clegg, A (2013) *Continuous Provision in the Early Years*. London: Bloomsbury.

Carr, M (2001) *Assessment in Early Childhood Settings: Learning Stories*. London: Paul Chapman.

Carr, M and Claxton, G (2002) Tracking the development of learning dispositions. *Assessment in Education, 9*(1): 9–37.

Dahlberg, G and Moss, P (2005) *Ethics and Politics in Early Childhood Education*. London: Routledge.

Department for Children, Schools and Families (2008) *The Statutory Framework for the Early Years Foundation Stage*. Nottingham: DCSF.

Department for Education (2017) *Statutory Framework for the Early Years Foundation Stage: Setting the Standards for Learning, Development and Care for Children from Birth to Five*. London: DfE.

Dubiel, J (2016) *Effective Assessment in the Early Years Foundation Stage*. London: Sage.

Dyer, M and Firth, N (2018) Being a reflective practitioner, in McMahon, S and Dyer, M (eds) *Work-based Practice in the Early Years: A Guide for Students*. Abingdon: Routledge.

Early Education (2012) *Development Matters in the Early Years Foundation Stage (EYFS)*. London: Early Education. Available at https://www.foundationyears.org.uk/wp-content/uploads/2012/03/Development-Matters-FINAL-PRINT-AMENDED.pdf

Ellis, Y G, Cliff, D P and Okely, A D (2018) Childcare educators' perceptions of and solutions to reducing sitting time in young children: A qualitative study. *Early Childhood Education Journal, 46*: 377.

Frampton, I, Jenkin, R and Waters, P (2015) Researching the benefits of the outdoor environment for children, in Hay, S (ed), *Early Years Education and Care*. Abingdon: Routledge, pp125–38.

Garhart Mooney, C (2000) *Theories of Childhood: An Introduction to Dewey, Montessori, Erikson, Piaget and Vygotsky*. St Paul, MN: Redleaf Press.

Giske, R, Ugelstad, I B, Meland, A T, Kaltvedt, E H, Eikeland, S, Finn, E T and Reikerås, E K L (2018) Toddlers' social competence, play, movement skills and well-being: An analysis of their relationship based on authentic assessment in kindergarten. *European Early Childhood Education Research Journal, 26*(3): 362–74.

Glazzard, J, Chadwick, D, Webster, A and Percival, J (2010) *Assessment for Learning in the Early Years Foundation Stage*. London: Sage.

Jasper, M (2013) *Beginning Reflective Practice* (2nd edn). Andover: Cengage Learning.

Johnston, J (2013) Enabling environments, in Beckley, P (ed) *Learning in Early Childhood*. London: Sage, pp137–47.

Laevers, F (2000) Forward to basics! Deep-level learning and the experiential approach. *Early Years, 20*(2): 20–9.

Shoval, E, Sharir, T and Arnon, M (2018) The effect of integrating movement into the learning environment of kindergarten children on their academic achievements. *Early Childhood Education Journal, 46*: 355.

Sylva, K, Melhuish, E, Sammons, P, Siraj-Blatchford, I and Taggart, B (2004) *The Effective Provision of Pre-School Education (EPPE) Project*. London: DfES.

UNICEF (1989) *The United Nations Convention on the Rights of the Child (UNCRC)*. London: UNICEF.

Warden, C (2016) *Learning with Nature: Embedding Outdoor Practice*. London: Sage.

Wardle, L and Vestey, S (2015) Exploring children's well-being and motivations, in Woods, A (ed), *The Characteristics of Effective Learning: Creating and Capturing the Possibilities in Early Years*. Abingdon: Routledge.

SECTION 3

PLANNING FOR AGES AND STAGES

7 PLANNING FOR BABIES AND TODDLERS

BIRTH TO 23 MONTHS

Kate Banfield and Angela Sugden

CHAPTER AIMS

By the end of this chapter you will be able to:

- explain how babies and toddlers learn
- understand the developmental needs of babies and toddlers
- consider how to plan for babies and toddlers within the EYFS
- start to develop a learning environment that supports the developmental needs of babies and toddlers in the EYFS

INTRODUCTION

The evidence shows that lasting and important attitudes to learning are shaped early, and many crucially during babyhood.

(Pascal and Bertram, 2000, p1)

In setting the scene for this chapter, we would like to reiterate the message from Chapter 1 that the non-statutory guidance, *Development Matters in the Early Years Foundation Stage* (Early Education, 2012), and the statements within it, are intended to be a guide for assessment and not a planning tool. The statements provide an overview of typical progression of children's learning in broad bands of development from birth to 5 years. Stewart (2016), who co-authored *Development Matters*, is very clear in her paper, 'Development Matters: A landscape of possibilities, not a roadmap', that the statements are not to be used as a linear next step list of skills and learning tasks that babies and toddlers must achieve. This is reminiscent of teaching to the test. If used in this way, this can severely limit the development and learning potential of the youngest children in our care and the experiences and learning opportunities that we offer them. Therefore, when planning for babies' and toddlers' ongoing learning and development it is important to remember that we need to use all our knowledge of how babies and toddlers learn and develop, use what we know from our observations, along with what parents and carers tell us. In addition, if working with colleagues we should also note what they share with us during professional dialogue about their observations of babies' and toddlers' development.

THE UNIQUE CHILD

REFLECTION ACTIVITY 7.1

The Unique Child is the starting place for all our planning.

Consider for a moment what children from birth to 2 years are like.

Make a list of skills and competences they develop during this time.

A new-born baby is totally dependent on the adult to provide them with what they need. They are driven to quickly develop their understanding of the world they are born into. They are learning from birth, if not before. Babies and toddlers are explorers, on a mission to make discoveries and learn. They develop new skills and knowledge rapidly during the first two years of life. Babies are born curious, they have an inborn disposition to understand and engage with their world. Their learning is active, persistent and sustained. Babies and toddlers are experiential learners who are intrinsically motivated and display from birth the Characteristics of Effective Learning, as described in the EYFS (DfE, 2017, p10). They are explorers and discoverers, not producers. Babies and toddlers cannot make and produce such things as cards for their special people, egg box daffodils or hedgehog pictures.

HOW DO BABIES AND TODDLERS LEARN?

BRAIN DEVELOPMENT

Babies and young children have powerful learning mechanisms that allow them to spontaneously revise, reshape, and restructure their knowledge. Babies' brains change as a result of the new things that they learn about the world (Gopnik et al., 1999). At birth, neural pathways are still waiting to be formed. Playful experiences and interactions with the environment begin to give information to babies and toddlers for the strengthening of these pathways. Most of the 100 billion neurons that babies are born with are not connected in networks. Connections among neurons are formed as the growing child experiences the surrounding world (Shore, 1997).

✓   **TIPS FOR PRACTICE**

Remember babies and non-walkers need access to the outdoor environment. This can be visually stimulating with plants, flowers, bird feeders, shiny mobiles, ribbons and wind chimes. Provide objects at different levels, for example on the floor and hanging from above, vary the objects and provide different colours, textures and sounds to grasp at.

THEORIES ON LEARNING

In the nineteenth century Friedrich Froebel (1897) in his kindergartens was advocating play and first-hand learning experiences for young children. He was a man who enjoyed nature and the outdoors, and was sensitive to the educational needs of children. He encouraged the development of the whole child. He promoted the view that the physical world, the garden and objects are crucial to experiential learning and to the development of the 'free' spirit in children. 'The garden was also a central aspect of the environment and contextual side of education and experience' (Bruce et al., 1995, p31). This philosophy informs us that what babies, toddlers and young children need are outdoor experiences where they can move freely, explore and make discoveries. They need 'real' meaningful experiences that are in context. Children learn by doing and acting on their environment.

Jean Piaget (1954), in his theory of cognitive development, named the first stage of his four-stage model as the sensorimotor stage of development. The sensorimotor stage of development lasts from birth to around 2 years of age. In the simplest of terms, babies learn through their senses and through movement. Piaget believed that a new-born baby is capable of integrating with the world in quite a specific way, which in his view ensures progressive adaptation to the world. Initially, action in the new-born is limited to a set of reflexes, but gradually as they become older and more practised they form more complex activities. The sensorimotor structures are the basis for their later cognitive development. Our senses are our guide through the world around us and for babies and toddlers they provide endless opportunity for fascinating discovery.

REFLECTION ACTIVITY 7.2

Froebel and Piaget remind us that babies' and toddlers' learning is maximised when we plan opportunities for them to move freely and to explore everyday resources and their outdoor environment. Consider the planning in your setting or in a placement setting that you have experienced. Can you identify planned opportunities that supported children to move freely and to explore the everyday and natural resources in their environment? What might you provide to further enhance the provision?

PLAY

There is no clear definition of play. It is most often described as a set of behaviours that suggest play, or suggestions of what play is not. Nevertheless, there is a general consensus internationally that play is the natural vehicle for learning for all mammals, including humans. Play for babies and toddlers is an important avenue for learning. While 'playing', babies and toddlers are learning about themselves, where they end and where they begin. They also learn about other people and the world around them (Manning-Morton and Thorpe, 2003). Play for babies and toddlers should not be divided into compartments of time to play and time for other things. The important care routines are just as valuable a play experience as playing with water in a tray. This should be so in all settings.

HOLISTIC DEVELOPMENT

As already discussed in Chapter 1, the requirements of the EYFS are to focus strongly on supporting babies and toddlers in the prime areas of learning, but not exclusively. It is important when planning for babies' and toddlers' learning and development that we have an understanding of their holistic development. Holistic development means that all areas of learning function and develop as a whole at the same time. Babies and toddlers do not compartmentalise their learning as we may do, but they use their skills and understanding from all areas of learning as they explore and discover, and they do this all at the same time. When providing play experiences for babies, it is vitally important that we fully understand the learning potential of what we provide, not only across the prime areas of learning, but also across the specific areas of learning. For example, when babies and toddlers explore the cornflour, sand or autumn leaves they experience the therapeutic qualities of these materials; they vocalise and talk while the adult may introduce new words to help build their vocabulary. They develop their manipulative skills, body strength and coordination as they balance and handle the materials; they learn to focus their listening in preparation for hearing the sounds in words. They learn about quantities, heavy and light, how many and different shapes; they experience the world around them and develop their understanding of how materials change. They experience nature around them, and display their own ideas and creativity as they explore the materials in their own way. Quite simply, if we really consider what we provide for babies and toddlers and think about the learning possibilities, it is quite likely that whatever we provide will support their development in some way across many, if not all areas of learning.

CASE STUDY 7.1

Observation of Reggie

In this example, the practitioner sensitively responds to the baby and teaches in the moment, across several areas of learning.

Reggie, who is 8 months old, sits on the practitioner's knee watching an older child play with oats. The practitioner holds him closely, rocks him gently and talks to him soothingly as she helps him to come around from his sleep. When he is fully alert the practitioner offers Reggie a tray containing oats to feel and explore. Reggie tentatively holds out his hands and then pulls back demonstrating a little insecurity. The practitioner talks to him reassuringly and encouragingly, supporting his confidence. She holds the oats in her own hands and demonstrates how to feel them. The practitioner talks to him sensitively about a similar experience he has had when touching his own dinner. Reggie looks at the practitioner and listens attentively to her voice. The practitioner gives wonderful eye contact, reassures him and offers an encouraging manner that gives him the confidence to hold out his hands and touch the oats. The practitioner praises and encourages him further. She carefully places him in a sitting position beside the tray of oats. The practitioner respectfully asks, 'Shall we take your socks off, so that you can feel the oats with your feet?' The practitioner pours the oats gently over Reggie's feet, checking constantly for his reaction. Reggie puts out his hands to touch and swipe the oats and also takes some to his mouth to taste. Reggie vocalises excitedly. The practitioner responds in a high sing-song voice asking, 'How does that feel, Reggie?' She leaves time and space for him to respond. Reggie vocalises again and seems to be expressing his delight. The practitioner narrates what he is doing and talks to him using a high sing-song voice stating, 'I haven't heard you use those sounds before'. Reggie leans over and continues to grasp the oats and spends time letting them flow through his hands. He excitedly articulates sounds and moves his hands expressively across the tray of oats. He displays his growing confidence in his explorations.

The practitioner displayed her loving care for Reggie and absolute sensitivity to his needs and was incredibly tuned-in to his verbal and non-verbal communication. This illustrates the importance of a key person and consistent relationship. The practitioner's relationship with Reggie represents what Page (2011) describes as, 'professional love'. The practitioner effectively used her knowledge of child development and of Reggie to successfully teach him, and expand his experience and confidence to explore. She displayed and used her knowledge of babies as sensory learners in providing the oats during the highly sensitive interaction, and showed her understanding of how Reggie was feeling and what he was interested in. The practitioner gauged Reggie's level of confidence and scaffolded his learning particularly well. She skilfully responded in the moment, and planned and adapted her teaching simultaneously to extend his learning and experience. The practitioner was very sensitive but offered challenge. Her teaching had an immediate impact on Reggie's learning and development. She was sitting close by and offered reassurance. She gave Reggie plenty of time to sustain his concentration. In her reflection on the experience, the practitioner explained that she asked Reggie if she could take his shoes off as she felt that touching the material with his feet was less threatening for him. Throughout the interaction the practitioner displayed her absolute dedication to supporting Reggie's learning and development. As Page reminds us, 'Young children flourish when they are in the company of adults who are genuinely interested in them and are able to form strong, attuned attachment relationships with them' (Page, 2015, p16).

REFLECTION ACTIVITY 7.3

How has the practitioner tailored this learning activity to the individual needs of the child?

(Continued)

In the observation, Reggie displays a secure attachment and trust with his special adult in the setting. He displays his growing confidence in his exploration of the oats, showing that he feels safe and secure in the practitioner's care. Reggie vocalises and displays his understanding of how to hold a conversation and shows his ability to take turns during interactions. Reggie develops balance, coordination and control of his body as he reaches out to explore and develops growing muscle strength in his hands as he grasps the oats and lets them flow through his hands to let them go. He will need muscle strength in his hands when he comes to write in later years (Macintyre, 2007). Reggie is learning about capacity and speed as he grasps the oats and lets them flow through his hands. During his exploration of the oats Reggie is developing his understanding of the world around him and how materials behave. Reggie uses his body expressively and makes marks and patterns as he explores the oats. With regard to displaying the Characteristics of Effective Learning, Reggie was actively playing with, and exploring the qualities of the oats. He showed his confidence in having a go, concentrated well and persisted in his exploration of the oats. Reggie developed his own ideas, and was active in his discovery of how he could change the oats by moving his hands through them. He was also building on what he already knew as he explored the oats using his mouth.

From this short observation it is clear that Reggie is progressing well in his learning and development. He is operating securely in the age band 8–20 months, but is beginning to demonstrate some of the statements in the 16–26 months age band. However, using a best fit approach from the information gained through the observation, we would suggest a summative assessment of 8–20 months, which is typical for his age. Of course, the practitioner would know much more about Reggie than the short observation informs us, so it may be that he is operating above his expected levels of development. This clearly illustrates that the practitioner's knowledge, both of child development and of Reggie, enabled her to provide an experience that, while being age and stage appropriate, also challenged him as an individual to make progress in the moment.

PLANNING FOR BABIES AND TODDLERS

It is important to understand that planning for babies and toddlers is not just about providing different activities for them. Keep in mind that the whole world is new to them, and babies are not bored. It is our job to provide them with thoughtful, broad and relevant experiences to help them learn about the world. Planning for their individual needs and learning should commence before they start to attend our setting. Dialogue with their parents and carers is essential to capture the fullest picture of the baby's or toddler's personality and levels of development. Getting to know babies and toddlers is more than taking information from parents and carers about their child's likes and dislikes or just the prime areas of learning. This is reiterated in the Early Years inspection handbook (2018, p38) 'Parents contribute to initial assessments of children's starting points on entry'. Therefore, this, along with your observations of babies and toddlers, will help you to tailor their care and education from the very beginning.

✓ **TIPS FOR PRACTICE**

For many reasons some babies and toddlers have less support available from their parents. You can help parents to develop their knowledge and confidence of how to support their children by:

- setting aside space for parents to play with their child for as little as 10 minutes before they go to work and have a staff member available to help with play ideas
- inviting them to a pre-arranged sing-a-long with their baby or toddler and provide words to nursery rhymes and songs
- providing them with ideas and resources to try activities at home
- showcasing simple and inexpensive sensory activities using, for example, found materials such as leaves and twigs, oats, pasta and items destined for recycling
- providing information about free/low cost activities in the local area

FOUR KEY DIMENSIONS OF THE CONTINUOUS CURRICULUM

In planning for babies and toddlers we need to consider four key dimensions of the continuous curriculum:

- emotional;
- how we treat each other;
- physical space, experiences and resources;
- adult/child interactions.

Emotional

This dimension concerns the key person role and how this impacts on the emotional well-being of babies, toddlers, parents and staff. Goldschmied (1994) developed the key person approach which was grounded in the need for babies, toddlers and young children to be provided with personalised care and learning experiences. Goldschmied held the view that the implementation of a key person approach strengthened relationships, creating a triangle of care between parents, key person and the babies and toddlers that were cared for. A key person for babies, toddlers and young children is now enshrined in law within the *Statutory Framework for the Early Years Foundation Stage* (DfE, 2017). It is both a learning and development requirement and a safeguarding and welfare requirement. 'The key person must help ensure that every child's learning and care is tailored to meet their individual needs' (DfE, 2017, p10).

REFLECTION ACTIVITY 7.4

Think about a time when you went into an unfamiliar environment such as a new Nursery, or a new school or a new job.

Now consider how having a special person looking out for you in these situations would impact on your sense of well-being and reduce stress.

Imagine important people in your life disappearing every year, or every few months – or brothers and sisters or friends. How would you feel? Consider what it is like for babies and toddlers as they move into different rooms within the Nursery.

We can best understand and empathise with a young child by drawing on our own experience as adults. As most of us cannot remember much before the age of three, this is one of the few ways available to us of attempting to understand the sensations and feelings of a small child and developing an empathetic approach to their emotional and social needs.

How we treat each other

This dimension concerns the organisational culture of the setting with regards to how adults talk to and listen to each other, resolve conflict and support each other. Things to consider in this dimension are policies and relationships that involve working in partnership with parents, your welcoming approach, equal opportunities and diversity, team building, supervision and behaviour management. It is important to remember that how adults behave and respond to children and each other is part of the curriculum. This too, requires thoughtful planning and evaluation, as it directly influences the children's learning and development. Adults are role models for babies and toddlers, who learn through watching and experiencing your interaction, both with them and with their parents and colleagues. This is part of what we call the hidden curriculum, and often gives us clear messages about what it is like for children and others. Without this even being spoken about, we often notice how a setting feels.

Physical space, experiences and resources

Meeting the needs of babies and toddlers can be difficult to manage, but planned areas of continuous provision along with open-ended materials provide them with appropriate levels of stimulation and learning experiences. It is important to recognise the importance of continuous provision and consider such an environment as an entitlement in our work with babies and toddlers. In providing continuous provision for babies and toddlers it is to be noted that all resources, environments and displays should reflect and meet the needs of the wider community, ethnicity and additional needs. It is important to remember that babies and young children need to have time to wallow in materials to fully understand them and therefore it is an important plan for materials to stay out a number of days at a time, rather than having something different every day. Gandini (1998) reminds us that in the Reggio Emilia nurseries of northern Italy, Malaguzzi emphasised that great care is taken in preparing the environment, and he defined it as the third teacher.

Adult/child interactions

This dimension concerns the learning and teaching that takes place as a result of observation, assessment and planning. Babies and toddlers need adults to be involved with them and their play. Adult/child interactions are best supported when adults are playing alongside children on the floor and are following the babies' and toddlers' lead in the activity that they want to pursue. The adult should sing and talk to the babies, engage in 'parent ease', which is using a high sing-song voice and taking turns in conversation. They need to model playing with the cornflour, building the train tracks or cooking in the home bay. The adult role is to be observant, interested and engaged with the babies and toddlers, offering plenty of opportunities for them to explore materials first hand and scaffold and support their learning and skills. It is difficult to plan in advance for this dimension of the continuous curriculum, so practitioners find that they plan 'in the moment', making instant choices about how to respond to babies and toddlers, how to challenge them, provide new possibilities, scaffold learnings, model skills and engage in sustained shared thinking. However, without a nurturing relationship, close observation and a stimulating, well-planned learning environment, planning in the moment will be difficult to engage in and much less effective.

REFLECTION ACTIVITY 7.5

Think about these four key dimensions of planning for the continuous curriculum:

1. The emotional dimension
2. The way we treat each other
3. The physical spaces, experiences and resources
4. The adult/child interactions

Which dimension stands out to you as an area of strength in your work or placement setting? Which dimension is an area for development?

THE PURPOSE OF CHILD-CENTRED PLANNING

We plan so that we can be sure to provide a curriculum that is broad, balanced and appropriate, and to ensure that we cover what we want babies and toddlers to learn, while taking account of their development levels. Planning for babies and toddlers should come from our observations of them and what we know about child development. We use our knowledge of how babies and toddlers learn and develop and their predictable interests, as well as what is happening around them. Being alert to and responsive in our teaching to what captures their interest is important. However, if we plan only for babies' and toddlers' interests, then the experiences that we provide can become narrow and our curriculum may become impoverished rather than enriching, as it should be. Consider how frequently a baby's focus, interest and enquiry changes in the course of a day, an hour and even a minute.

A young baby of 9 months will possess an innate drive to move, communicate, explore, discover and develop. They may be interested in pulling themselves up, while at the same time be fascinated by the reflection of light on the carpet. But, you know that one of their predictable interests will be filling and emptying. You will add reflective items that they have to either reach up for or sit down with. It may also be winter and you may use this opportunity to provide unique experiences such as exploring snow, which would not have been an interest of theirs, as they would not have seen it before, and those older babies that have experienced snow will not remember. This is why it is important to use all your knowledge of child development, age and stage of development, and predictable interests, as well your observations and information from parents about what babies and toddlers are especially interested in.

THE PLANNING PROCESS

With all of the information provided in the chapter thus far, you may wish to consider the process shown in Figure 7.1, which illustrates the stages of child-centred planning.

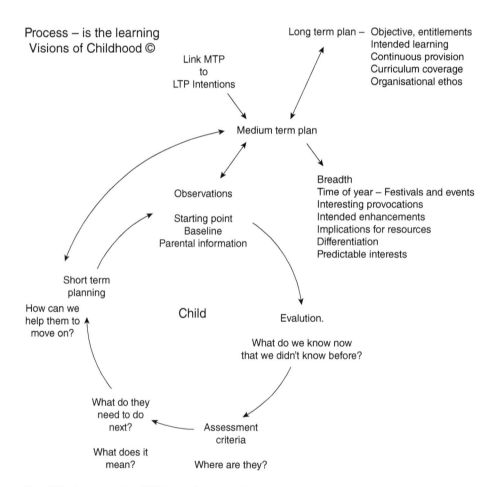

Key: LTP = long term plan, MTP = medium term plan

Figure 7.1   The stages of child-centred planning

Long-term planning

Long-term planning helps you to provide a well-structured and rich learning environment. Long-term planning is concerned with the learning opportunities and the continuous provision that you wish the babies and toddlers to access across a defined time such as a year. The long-term plan underpins all other planning processes and includes the following:

- the aims and objectives of the setting;
- an overview of the topics and areas of learning to be covered over the year;
- the rationale for learning opportunities, resources and experiences;
- the rationale for learning opportunities through everyday routines such as meal times and changing babies and toddlers;
- partnership with parents;
- the process of observation and assessment;
- the role of the adult in the care, teaching and learning;
- policies and procedures that guide practice and support babies' and toddlers' experiences.

Medium-term planning

Medium-term planning is often forgotten about when planning for babies and toddlers. The medium-term plan covers a period of time of about six weeks or a term. It allows for the continuum of learning and depth of experience. In the medium-term plan you identify specific threads from the overall curriculum to focus on and work with in detail. In addition, it allows you to be able to consider festivals and events, specific learning needs, organisation and responsibility. Also the medium term is good to share with parents as they can support the overall intention of the learning outcomes with their child. It should include details such as:

- the focus or theme if used;
- the focus areas of learning and the learning intentions;
- opportunities, experiences and enhancements;
- resources and differentiation;
- the role of the adult;
- the period of time it covers;
- evaluation.

Differentiation for the different ages and stages of babies and the challenges of those older babies can be seen in Tables 7.1–7.4. As identified in the medium-term planning example shown in Table 7.1, the planning for the youngest children is very sensory and experiential, whereas for the older children it is more concept driven. Both age groups are experiencing and learning about spring in ways that make sense to them, and building on what has been learned and experienced before. In this way, babies and toddlers build up a strong store of knowledge, concepts and skills that they use to make sense of their experiences and their environment.

Table 7.1 Example medium-term plan

	Youngest children	Older children
What is the theme?	Soil, frogs, water, butterflies, flowers, mini beasts	Growth, spring, change, mini beasts
When will it happen?	April, May, June	
Focus	Senses: smell, taste, touch, sight and hearing Development: physical, emotional and social	Understanding the world Personal and social, communication, language and literacy, mathematics
Learning possibilities: What we/I want the children to understand	Cause and effect (that adding water to soil makes mud) Texture (dirt is dry, mud is wet) Naming life forms (flower, spider, ladybird, frog) Naming and emulating movement (wiggle, crawl, jump and hop) That flowers grow	The life cycle sequencing of growth, plant, mini beast or animal The environment those things need to grow Classification of life forms, i.e. is a beetle an insect or a plant? Cause and effect (what happens if you do not water a plant) Metamorphous (what it means)
How will we/I promote equal opportunities through this theme?	Pictures and books supporting positive images Access for all children to materials Celebrate appropriate festivals that occur in the duration of the theme Read stories where there are female leads	
How will we/I involve the children's parents in their learning?	Sharing information with parents: verbally, written, electronically	
What other resources do we/I have to put in place to support this theme?	Plants, seeds, soil, compost, digging equipment, plant pots, mini beasts (caterpillars, mealworms, ants, frogspawn)	
Evaluation What did or did not interest the children? What learning was observed?		

In the example shown in Table 7.2, the practitioner has used all areas and aspects of learning as a focus for the skills and concepts that she wants the babies and toddlers to experience and learn across a defined period of time. In addition, she has highlighted enhancements for additional resources to help ensure that the settings have the materials in place that will be needed to support learning.

Table 7.2 Example medium-term plan

Autumn Term: Sept–Dec – Baby room medium-term planning – prime areas of learning Topic: Autumn			
Area of learning		Learning objective/concept	Practice/provision/resource
Communication and language	Listening and attention	Sounds/words Turn taking	Music/musical instruments Singing Song sacks Peek a boo
	Understanding	Following simple instructions with hand gestures Simple situational directions (body parts)	Makaton Singing/songs: Head, shoulders, knees and toes
	Speaking	Babbling Single words	Narration Repetitiveness of singular words/object names Singing/songs: Head, shoulders, knees and toes, Twinkle twinkle little star, Wind the bobbin up, Miss Polly had a dolly
Personal, social, emotional development	Self-confidence and self-awareness	Awareness of self-identity	Mirrors Child's box/photos of self/family Singing: Head, shoulders, knees and toes
	Making relationships	Building a relationship with key person Peers	Key person system Group activities Communication friendly space: tepee
	Managing feelings and behaviour	Empathy Turn taking	Modelling empathy Peek a boo Home corner: babies/dolls
Physical development	Moving and handling: fine motor skill	Palmer grasp/pincer grasp Object permanence Mature finger grasp Mature release of objects	Smaller objects: conkers, pine cones, sticks Heuristic materials: wooden blocks, lids etc. Model: pinching, pointing, rolling, placing objects

(Continued)

Table 7.2 (Continued)

| | Moving and handling: gross motor skills | Rolling

Crawling

Pulls to standing

Independent walking

Emerging hand preference | Tunnel

Large-scale painting – (easel/window/garden painting – mud kitchen) object – rollers, paintbrushes, sticks

Outside: wooden blocks – assault courses, different heights, climbing arch, walkers, push along bikes, tunnel |
| | Health and self-care | Feeding with spoon

Holding beaker cup

Drinking from cup

Potty training

Assists with dressing | Modelling and encouraging at lunchtime, snack times

Nappy changing time discussion wet/soiled

Winter clothing: coat, hat, gloves etc. |

Autumn Term: Sept–Dec – Baby room medium-term planning – specific areas of learning Topic: Autumn/winter			
Area of learning		Learning objective/ concepts	Resource/activity
Literacy	Reading	Love of reading material with interest	Autumn poems Books in continuous provision Story sacks
	Writing	Explore making marks	**Edible paints:** Autumn colours **Cornflour:** Autumn enhancements – scent, colour, collections (conkers etc.).
Maths	Numbers	One to one principle	All resources in continuous provision
	Shape, space and measure	Many/few Full/empty Basic shapes High/low Big/little On/under	**Water play:** Autumn colours, scent, collection enhancements Heuristic materials Wooden blocks Peek a boo/parachute games
Understanding the world	People and communities	Themselves Familiar people Local area	Mirrors Photos books/child boxes Song: Head, shoulders, knees and toes Care routines Key person: boxes Local area trips: shops, park, nature reserve

	The world	Hot/cold Light/dark Season: Autumn Animals/wildlife	**Water play:** warm water/frozen Outside play Walking in nature reserve/woods Light box/light toys **Enhanced provision:** nature walks, sensory bottles, autumn tray Nature walks
	Technology	Light/dark On/off Cause and effect	Light toys Technology resources
Expressive arts and design	Exploring media and materials	Soft/hard Loud and quiet	**Smell:** Cinnamon, berries, orange, sage, frankincense, ginger in dough, cornflour, water. Scent bags **Texture:** Crunchy, crisp, smooth – leaves, sticks, conkers, pine cones, oranges, sage, cornflour, water, frozen ice, treasure baskets **Taste:** Orange, cinnamon, ginger, pumpkin, butternut squash. Autumn/winter menu. **Hear:** Birds, wind, leaves – walks **Songs:** Autumn song – Autumn leaves Twinkle twinkle little star, Head, shoulders, knees and toes **Music:** Musical instruments **Colours:** Brown, yellow, red, green. Black and white area **Movement/dance:** Autumn leaves song actions. Head, shoulders, knees and toes, Movement sticks **Art:** Edible paints – scents and matching colours of autumn/winter, leaf painting, and painting with sticks **Role play:** Home kitchen – food taste, scent exploration tray
	Being imaginative	Imitate everyday actions from experiences	Daily routines Home corner Babies/dolls

Medium-term plans developed by Chloe Marsden at Sunshine Day Nursery, Huntington, York.

Short-term planning

Short-term planning allows you to meet individual babies' and toddlers' current interests and learning requirements. This information will have been gained from your observations and discussions with parents and colleagues. You use what you know about children to plan experiences to support and extend their learning and development. Having said that, it also needs to be flexible, so that you are able to respond spontaneously to follow babies' and toddlers' particular ideas as they present themselves. Short-term planning is where the strongest link between assessment and planning is forged. You draw on your in-depth knowledge of the babies and toddlers, including where they are in their learning and development. Think back to the observation of Reggie and the practitioner. The teaching was tailored in the moment to meet Reggie's needs and interests. The written plan for Reggie identified adding sensory materials, including the oats as part of his next steps in learning in order to expand his understanding of everyday materials. Hutchin (2000) reminds us that as practitioners we need to be clear about what is appropriate for the child to move on to next, whether this is the next developmental stage such as encouraging a baby to pull themselves up on sturdy furniture or for an older toddler to develop a particular skill such as putting on their own Wellington boots. Your short-term plans may not necessarily be recorded on paper, but may be written on the white board or planning board, so that in the absence of a key person, babies' and toddlers' individual learning and development continues to be supported and tailored by a significant other person. As identified in the two planning pro-forma examples, Tables 7.3 and 7.4, the planning is tailored to the individual learning priorities and what next for individual babies and toddlers.

Table 7.3 Example short-term plan for an individual baby or toddler

Name of child:	Week commencing/Date:
From our observations, assessments, discussions with parents and colleagues – what are the learning priorities or next steps for the baby or toddler? (This might include developmental needs, what you want them to know and learn and their interests such as schemas) • • •	
What play and learning experiences will be provided to support the learning priorities for the baby or toddler? • • •	
What is the role of the adult in supporting the baby's or toddler's learning and development? • • •	
Evaluation (implications for planning – what do we need to do next for the baby or toddler in order to support ongoing progress?)	

The weekly planning shown in Table 7.4 is completed by each individual key person with a focus on planning to meet the individual learning and next steps of each baby or toddler. Focusing the planning on each individual helps to ensure that provision is set up to meet the needs of that individual and the babies' and toddlers' personal interests can be explored.

It is quite a simple planning document which this setting finds to be effective in maximising the time that the practitioners have to work with the babies and toddlers, and impacts on their learning and development. The first column identifies what the activity is so it can be tailored to each individual's interest, area of learning or next step. The second column is why? What is the purpose of the activity or experience? This column has been designed to help the practitioners to really think about why they are providing the activity or experience and what they aim to teach the baby or toddler. The third column is for the practitioners to reflect and evaluate the learning that has taken place.

The last column encourages the practitioner to use what they know about the child and their learning to develop a forward plan or 'what next?'

Table 7.4 Example short-term plan for an individual baby or toddler

Weekly planning				
Week commencing: Member of staff:				Name of child
	What?	**Why?** What is the purpose of the activity?	**Assess** What learning has taken place?	**Next step** What are you going to do next?
Monday				
Tuesday				
Wednesday				
Thursday				
Friday				

Short-term plan developed by Sarah Bambury of Greenhedges day Nursery, Scarborough.

CONCLUSION

This chapter has explored how babies and toddlers learn and develop. It has highlighted the benefits of planning holistically for babies and toddlers, taking into account their need to move freely and explore their natural environments. It draws on Froebel's advocacy for outdoor learning and Piaget's constructivist theory, to present the case for child-centred planning based on four key dimensions of the continuous curriculum: the emotional dimension, the way we treat each other, the physical environment, experiences and resources and the adult/child interactions. Advice is given on planning for long-term provision, medium-term foci and short-term learning experiences. These were illustrated through examples of short-term planning from different practitioners, which demonstrate that there is no set way for planning for babies and toddlers. Rather, there is an argument presented for personalised planning, which is flexible and meaningful to the practitioners who record it and which addresses the prior learning and ongoing development of the babies and toddlers for whom it is intended to support.

FURTHER READING

Burns, C (n.d.) Tummy Time. Available at: www.mamabebe.org/spiral-of-development/tummy-time/
Gerdhart, S (2004) *Why Love Matters: How Affection Shapes a Baby's Brain*. London: Routledge.
Robinson, M (2003) *Birth to One*. Maidenhead: Open University Press.
Zero to Three. Available at: www.zerotothree.org

REFERENCES

Bruce, T, Findlay, A, Read, J and Scarborough, M (1995) *Recurring Themes in Education*. London: Paul Chapman Publishing.
Department for Education (2017) *Statutory Framework for the Early Years Foundation Stage*. London: DfE.
Early Education (2012) *Development Matters in the Early Years Foundation Stage (EYFS)*. London: Early Education. Available at https://www.foundationyears.org.uk/wp-content/uploads/2012/03/Development-Matters-FINAL-PRINT-AMENDED.pdf
Froebel, F (1897) *The Education of Man*. Translated by William T Harris (1911). New York and London: D. Appleton & Company.
Gandini, L (1998) Educational and caring spaces, in Edwards, C, Gandini, G and Forman, G (eds) *The Hundred Languages of Children: The Reggio Emilia Approach – Advanced Reflections* (2nd edn). Greenwich, CT: Ablex Publishing Corporation.
Goldschmied, E (1994) *People Under Three*. New York: Routledge.
Gopnik, A, Meltzoff, A and Kuhl, P (1999) *How Babies Think*. London: Weidenfield & Nicholson/Orion Publishing.
Hutchin, V (2000) *Tracking Significant Achievement in the Early Years* (2nd edn). London: Hodder & Stoughton.
Macintyre, C (2007) *Understanding Children's Development in the Early Years*. London: Routledge.
Manning-Morton, J and Thorpe, M (2003) *Key Times for Play*. Maidenhead: Open University Press.
Page, J (2011) Do mothers want professional carers to love their babies? *Journal of Early Childhood Research*, 9(3): 310–23.
Page, J (2015) *Love, Love, Love*. London: Nursery World, MA Education.
Pascal, C and Bertram, T (2000) *Further Memorandum from The Effective Early Learning Project (EY 82) Accounting Early for Life Long Learning: The Importance of Dispositions, Self and Emotional Well Being*, Professor Christine Pascal and Dr Tony Bertram. Select Committee on Education and Employment Minutes of Evidence, 12 July 2000. London: Parliamentary copyright.
Piaget, J (1954) *The Construction of Reality in the Child*. New York: Basic Books.
Shore, R (1997) *Rethinking the Brain*. New York: Families and Work Institute.
Stewart, N (2016) *A Landscape of Possibilities, Not a Road Map*. Lewes, East Sussex: Foundation Stage Forum.

8 PLANNING FOR 2-YEAR-OLDS

Kate Banfield and Angela Sugden

CHAPTER AIMS

By the end of this chapter you will be able to:

- understand the developmental and learning needs of children aged between 2 and 3 years
- consider the predictable interests and enquiry of 2-year-old children – schematic behaviour
- develop your practice in how you plan for children aged between 2 and 3 years
- understand how to develop the learning environment in order to support the developmental needs of 2-year-olds in the EYFS

INTRODUCTION

Play is a child's life and the means by which he comes to understand the world around him.

(Isaacs, 1933, p21)

In writing this chapter we wish to encourage you to consider the developmental needs of 2-year-olds and your expectations of children of this age. While we must have the highest expectations of what all children can achieve, this must be grounded in our understanding of child development. For example, we often expect 2-year-olds to sit in a group for circle time. Yet, many 2–3-year-olds struggle to sit and listen, in keeping with their sensory and physical maturation. They often become bored, fidgety and detached. This early formalisation of their learning ignores their drive to learn through play. Tassoni and Tassoni (2018) remind us that 2-year-old children will usually enjoy listening to a story shared with them individually or together with another child, but will find group circle time and group story time a challenge. This is because larger group activities are not always matched to the individual developmental needs of the children, particularly those aged between 2 and 3 years. Therefore, it is helpful to start this chapter by reminding ourselves of what a typical 2-year-old is like.

REFLECTION ACTIVITY 8.1

Think about 2-year-old children that you know.

Make a list of words that describe what they are like, and

Look through the Characteristics of Effective Learning on pages 6–7 in *Development Matters* (Early Education, 2012) and identify which characteristics they display at this stage of their development.

Often 2-year-old children are described in negative terms. For example, having temper tantrums or the 'terrible twos'. In thinking about 2-year-olds who are developing in line with typical expectations, we realise that they are *terrific*. Two-year-olds are likely to be physically active, show curiosity and be interested in people. They are explorers who are motivated to discover all sorts of things. Two-year-olds are fiercely independent, they make choices, are keen to 'have a go' and can follow their own ideas. But, equally they are intensely dependent, often fluctuating between independence and dependency. Two-year-olds are energetic, persistent, creative and resourceful. They review what works well and express their own views. They can communicate more expressively and use language with ever increasing fluency and complexity. In your list of what 2-year-olds are like, you may have used some of the following adjectives: playful, emotional, loving, mischievous, innovative, inquisitive, determined, adventurous, lively, imaginative and many more. Within the words that you used to describe children who are 2 years old it is likely that you will have identified how they display the Characteristics of Effective Learning as described in the EYFS.

TYPICAL 2-YEAR-OLDS

Children aged between 2 and 3 years begin to pretend more during play. They use familiar objects and situations to act out their experiences, such as making the tea, putting the baby to bed, playing shops or pretending to be the doctor. All of these skills and learning are supported by their fast-growing language skills and their questions of 'why?' and 'what is it?' over and over again.

In the year between the ages of 2 and 3, children develop their vocabulary and speaking skills extensively. They soak up the language rich environment that adults provide, adding newly acquired words to their play each day. By the age of 2, children typically display a vocabulary level of around 50 words; this rapidly increases to around 300 words by the time they are 3 years old.

Two-year-olds enjoy experimenting with open-ended resources and materials, which help them to develop confidence, achieve success and develop their creative thinking and ideas. They are developing their physical skills, cognition and personal characteristics that will help to ensure that they can access more formal literacy learning in later years. Two- to 3-year-olds enjoy books and stories being read to them, particularly as they snuggle up closely with their special adults. They will remember phrases from familiar stories and pretend to read, using their knowledge of favourite stories, as well as picture prompts to retell the stories that they know.

Two- to 3-year-olds typically enjoy singing songs and request their favourite songs with confidence. They remember the sequence of words and numbers, make marks and begin to emulate writing as they near 3 years of age. Some will recognise the initial letter of their name. They are interested and motivated to find out about nature and the world around them and they learn from older children, benefitting, whenever possible, from playing in mixed age groups.

HOW DO 2-YEAR-OLDS LEARN?

TYPICAL CHILD DEVELOPMENT

In order to think about how 2-year-olds learn, it is important to consider child development and have a thorough understanding of what would be considered to be development that is typical for children of this age. There are many text books with development charts that support us to know what is typical in terms of child development milestones. However, it is not a simplistic process in which all children routinely pass through each stage of development in a linear fashion. Consider the quote below, which reminds us that,

> Child development is a dynamic process of growth, transformation, learning and acquisition of abilities to respond and adapt to the environment in a planned, organised and independent manner. The process does not simply unfold with neurological maturation but is shaped positively or negatively, by the interactions between biological and environmental influences. These interactions result in a high level of variability in children's developmental outcomes. Learning about both the sequences of development and the context of development is necessary for understanding developmental progress.

(Sharma and Cockerill, 2014, p67)

Therefore, while it is important to have an understanding of the broad typical stages of development and be able to provide an environment, experiences and teaching that match typical development, it is also essential that practitioners tailor the environment, experiences and teaching to meet the specific developmental needs of the individual children.

REFLECTION ACTIVITY 8.2

How well do you know and understand the typical stages of development for children between the ages of 1 and 3 years? Rate yourself in the following areas (1 high to 5 low)

- social development
- physical development
- intellectual/cognitive development
- emotional development
- language development

The following options might help improve your knowledge and understanding. They are suggestions from students and practitioners who work with 2–3-year-olds:

- I bought a child development text book
- I discussed typical stages of development with my mentor on placement
- I worked with a colleague to make some charts to display in our room
- We asked our manager if there was any training we could attend and when there wasn't she provided a mini training session for us in a staff meeting. We all had to contribute by researching one aspect of development each and identifying four typical behaviours for our age group

BRAIN DEVELOPMENT

The 2-year-old's brain is developing at speed. The 100 billion brain cells that they were born with have been connecting up and continue to do this through making permanent pathways. Their brain cells connect up with each other as a result of the on-going repeated explorations and sensory learning experiences, along with the time they have with their parents, key people and other children. These experiences help 2-year-olds to develop their learning capacity and form the basis for lifelong learning.

> *In order for two year olds to become life-long learners and to be resilient, prepared, and motivated for future learning opportunities, the foundations for all parts of the brain need to be integrated and capable of working together. Part of this development is known as 'Executive Function', which includes working memory, inhibitory control and flexible thinking. This, alongside emotional regulation, provides the keys to open the doors of learning.*

(Fisher and Revels, 2014, p4)

For the 2-year-old who is developing executive functioning skills, the need for a stimulating play environment, consistent relationships and playful interactions with others are paramount.

PLAY

Duncan and Lockwood (2008) identify the different types of play that young children often enjoy. These are:

- exploratory or discovery play;
- imaginative play;
- physical play;
- play with natural materials;
- creative play; and
- outdoor play.

In planning the learning environments for 2-year-olds it is important for practitioners to consider the different types of play that they can engage with throughout the provision. During *exploratory or discovery* play children aged 2 years display their interest in what they can do with the play resources that practitioners provide for them. In this type of play we often see high levels of concentration. As young children explore they find out about the world around them.

If given the opportunity, 2–3-year-olds will act out familiar situations during their *imaginative play*. For example, if we provide empty packaging from cereals or toothpaste, and bread boxes children of this age with our support will pretend to play at shops and buy the things for sale in the shop. This will support their ever-growing language skills and develop their understanding of money. Children of this age will also act out situations such as pretending that their doll is poorly or pretending to make dinner in the play kitchen. Duncan and Lockwood (2008, p99) remind us that 'Imaginative play supports the development of areas of the brain related to such things as metacognition, problem solving, social cognition, literacy, mathematics and science'.

Two-year-olds display high levels of energy and during their *physical play* they continue to develop their physical competences, balance, coordination and body strength. It is important that practitioners provide 2-year-olds with opportunities to *play with natural materials* such as mud, sand and water to help them develop their understanding of the world around them. When combining sand and water, 2-year-olds develop their understanding of how natural materials change when mixed together. Two-year-olds develop their understanding of the seasons as they help to collect and explore the leaves that fall from the trees in autumn and discover the butterflies on the buddleia bush during the summer time.

Practitioners might describe most play for 2-year-olds as *creative play*. However, in this we are focusing on the opportunities we provide for them to display and express their own ideas when painting, drawing and model making with recycled materials. Too often, during creative activities 2-year-olds are encouraged to stick cotton wool on a pre-cut sheep to represent spring or stick shiny shapes on a pre-cut Christmas tree by well-meaning practitioners, but what this actually does is stifle young children's confidence in expressing their own creative ideas. Two-year-olds cannot yet draw the sheep or Christmas tree as competently as adults and this gives them a one-sided view about what something should look like when they re-create it. The Statutory Framework for the EYFS identifies three Characteristics of Effective Learning that practitioners must consider when 'planning and guiding children's learning'. One of these characteristics is, 'creating and thinking critically – children have and develop their own ideas, make links between ideas, and develop strategies for doing things' (DfE, 2017, p10). Therefore, as practitioners, we need to consider the developmental needs and interests of 2-year-olds and remember that not all of them will be interested in making identical things that are directed by adults.

An ideal environment for 2-year-olds to engage in all of these types of play is of course, the outdoor environment. Access to *outdoor play* is a legal requirement of the EYFS, 'Providers must provide access to an outdoor play area or, if that is not possible, ensure that outdoor activities are planned and taken on a daily basis (unless circumstances make this inappropriate, for example unsafe weather conditions)' (DfE, 2017, p30). Outdoor play supports 2-year-olds to develop their understanding of nature and the world around them, as well as helping to develop their physical competences, promoting their sense of well-being and much more.

✓ TIPS FOR PRACTICE

- provide open-ended play resources to promote creativity and imagination, for example, lengths of fabrics, cardboard tubes, milk crates, planks of wood etc.
- provide real resources as much as possible as this will support engagement and motivation
- provide unusual artefacts and resources to stimulate curiosity
- plan time and resources for 2-year-olds to regularly enjoy outdoor play

SCHEMAS

When planning for 2-year-olds, practitioners need to take into consideration a number of developmental tasks that young children need to engage in. Often this takes the form of schemas.

The concept of 'schema' is one way of looking at young children's learning and development, based on the theories of Piaget (1957) and developed more recently by Chris Athey (1991). The theory is that children learn through developing certain patterns of behaviour or 'schemas' which they use to organise their actions and thoughts. When involved in this process the child will repeat an action over and over again. For example, a young child interested in the concept of 'rotation' will investigate and explore using circular movements and show interest in round objects. Once the child knows the likely outcome of carrying out a particular action and how certain objects or materials are likely to behave, she/he will go on to explore a wider range of materials and experiences, gradually developing new schemas. As children develop, they do not lose any schemas but the ones they have are combined or integrated. Practitioners need to plan their provision needs to support children's schematic concerns and encourage their explorations further.

Arnold (2010, p21) reminds us that,

> It seems important to note that when we are thinking about extending thought in young children by 'feeding' their current schemas, we are thinking about the 'form' rather than the 'content'. Traditionally, in settings, we have been concerned with offering 'content' for example, to extend an interest in clocks, we might offer a range of timepieces 'related content'. Observation of the underlying 'form' might reveal an interest in rotation. Many more experiences could be offered to support and extend children's interest in rotation and circularity.

REFLECTION ACTIVITY 8.3

Think about the quote from Arnold (2010). Can you identify a time when you have focused on the 'content' of the schema rather than the 'form'?

Consider the scenario below:

A child is observed frequently pushing the toy cars so that they roll from one end of the room to the other. You notice the practitioner giving the child a wider selection of toy vehicles to play with and suggesting they use the garage in the small world area to park the cars up and pretend to fix them.

How might this practitioner focus on the 'form' of the schema rather than the 'content'?

CASE STUDY 8.1

Planning for schematic play

Samantha Clarke is a trainee Early Years Teacher (EYT) working in a pre-school for children aged 2 to 4 years. She describes how she has developed the planning in her setting to support children's schematic play and the impact it has had on children's learning:

> I began by asking staff to observe their key children and on a large display board place the children's initials next to the schema or schemas that they observed. We observed children over a period of two weeks, during which time I began the process of delivering information regarding schemas to children's parents and carers.

I identified that the majority of children who attend our setting were pursuing the following schemas: transporting, connecting, enclosing.

The *transporting schema* is the urge to transport things using hands, bags, containers. The area in which children chose to transport most items to and from was the home corner. I therefore began looking at what was available in that area to support a transporting schema, which was a minimal number of pans. I introduced resources including trays, shopping bags and prams. In conjunction with this I added a variety of different styles of bags, baskets, buckets that children could easily access, close to each of the areas.

The *enclosing schema* was identified from our observations of children being highly engrossed with the contents of the small world and sensory tray but often choosing to go under the tray with the resources. To support this, I attached a large sheet of material to the stand on which the tray sits to create a small den area and introduced a small bookstand to go inside with books that relate to the contents of the tray that day. Further to this, I introduced large building equipment and sheets of material that children could use to independently create their own dens. Staff have observed children actively engaging with each other to build their own dens and structures. Staff have then further extended on this and provided other opportunities to further develop children's learning.

A *connecting schema* is the fascination with connecting items together. We felt that the setting already provided a lot of resources that supported the connecting schema; however, we did identify that there were no opportunities for pursuing this schema in the water tray. This prompted me to introduce a water play area in which the children have access to a wide range of water play resources including different tubes, pipes, guttering and buckets that they can connect together.

Identifying children's schemas and introducing resources that support them has seen an increase in the number of children actively engaging in activities for longer periods of time. Staff have reported that children are wanting to join in activities, they are enthusiastic and curious. We have also seen an increase in children engaging with their peers in meaningful play, supporting each other and, when needed, asking staff for support rather than staff supporting children when they felt they needed it. When analysing the progress data for the autumn term, this is reflected in the increase in children progressing in not only their social skills, but also their communication skills. When I have analysed the observations produced by staff, I have noted that they are actively extending on children's interests and combining this with their individual schemas to support and challenge children's learning and development more effectively.

PLANNING FOR 2-YEAR-OLDS IN A CHILD-CENTRED WAY

From the previous section that has explored how 2-year-olds learn, it is evident that they are in a distinct phase of development that is different to babies and toddlers or, indeed, to 3- and 4-year-olds. It is important to remember, when planning for 2-year-olds, that they learn from everything that they encounter, both planned and unplanned. We must think carefully when planning for 2-year-olds and use all our knowledge of child development and learning theories to help us provide the best possible learning experiences and environment at the time they need it. Often practitioners are pressurised into providing a more formal approach to their curriculum, but it is important to resist this and provide each individual 2- and 3-year-old with what they need at this age, as it is these experiences that help to provide the strong foundations for their later, more formal learning.

NEEDS

Two-year-olds need support from practitioners who know them well, who tune in to their interests, learning and developmental needs. They need consistent and reliable feedback from their special adults about their actions. This type of feedback supports their social referencing, helps them to develop their understanding of social boundaries and helps them to develop empathy towards others. Case study 8.2 shows how one key person achieved this through planning in the moment (responding to what she knows about the child and what she observes) and through planning in partnership with the child's parents.

CASE STUDY 8.2

Longitudinal observation of Floyd and analysis of his learning

Floyd is 2-and-a-half years old and has been at Nursery in the 2–5s room for six months. He has very good language and understanding. He is confident, curious and motivated to learn. The Nursery have planned learning experiences and enhanced the environment based on the broad theme of spring. This includes planning to support children's learning about growth.

Floyd is very interested in planting and how the seed transforms into flowers or vegetables. His parents report that he points to trees and other shrubs and asks, 'Have they grew from seeds?' Floyd's key person observes his investigation in Nursery as he fills plant pots, looks for seeds and talks about the seeds in the apples. Floyd's favourite vegetables are peas. His key person uses her observations and all that she knows about Floyd's learning, development and interests to guide her planning and help him consolidate his learning about growth.

The key person asks Floyd if he would like to plant and grow some peas. Floyd shows excitement; the key person tells Floyd she has found a book about growing vegetables. Together they sit to look at the book and use the pictures to talk about the step by step process of growing peas. Floyd points to the pictures, identifying the seeds and putting them in the soil. The key person expands his understanding and vocabulary as she explains that this is called, 'sowing the seeds'. At the vegetable patch in the garden his key person explains how they need to dig the soil, then sieve the soil so that the seeds are able to grow.

Floyd uses the spade to dig, displaying body control and strength. His key person works alongside him. After finishing digging and sieving the soil, Floyd carefully plants the seeds in the rows of soil and gently covers them. His key person asks what else the peas will need to grow. Floyds talks knowledgeably about them needing the sun. His key person helps him to think about what else the seeds might need. She gives him time to consider her questions and after processing the information and thinking about his response he identifies that they need water. Floyd shows his independence as he uses the watering can to water the seeds.

Over the coming weeks, Floyd waters the seeds and shows great excitement when the plants start to appear. He is developing his language around planting and uses correct terminology as he proudly shows his mum the 'shoots' that are growing. As time goes on, his key person talks about the pea shoots needing sticks so that they can climb up and stay strong. They find the vegetable book again and look for the pictures to give them an idea of how long the sticks should be. Floyd finds some long doweling in the woodwork area. His key person asks him to think about how many centimetres long the sticks should be. Floyd says 10, showing his understanding of number. His key person helps him to measure 10 centimetres and then Floyd carefully uses the saw to cut along the line they have drawn. He knows about the rules of using the saw and holds his thumb close to his fingers. His key person suggests that they try this one to see if it is long enough, supporting his growing knowledge of estimation. Floyd takes the cut doweling outside and presses it into the ground. His key person uses questions to help him to think about whether the stick is long enough and how much taller the shoots may yet grow. Floyd decides that the stick needs to be much longer as the plants in the book look big. The key person expands on this well and introduces the mathematical concept of length.

As time goes on, Floyd continues to water the pea plants. One day as Floyd is checking his pea plants he runs to his key person full of excitement and says, 'the peas are growing'. His key person reinforces his understanding and describes how the pea pods have started to appear. A few weeks later they are a bit bigger. Floyd's key person supports his curiosity and asks if they should look inside one to see how the peas are growing in the pod. Floyd carefully detaches a pod and his key person teaches him how to split the pod carefully. Floyd quickly identifies that there are five little peas inside. His key person asks him if he thinks they are big enough to pick and eat yet. Floyd considers this and decides that they are not. He shows his understanding that the peas he eats are usually a bit bigger.

A few weeks later Floyd decides that the peas have grown enough and that they could pick them. Again, his key person uses this opportunity to add new vocabulary and explains that this is called 'harvesting' the peas. She brings him a bowl and says, 'We will need to shell them now, then we can eat some fresh from the pod and cook some for lunch'. Floyd uses good dexterity to pop the pods and remove the peas. He tastes one and comments, 'It's so sweet'. Floyds shares his peas with other staff and children. He shows his confidence as he explains the whole process from digging the soil, planting the seeds, caring for the peas as they grew and harvesting the peas.

In this case study Floyd's key person drew on her knowledge of Floyd, his family and her knowledge of child development and learning theories. In particular, she utilised Bruner's (1957) theory of learning and development to support and extend Floyd's knowledge and understanding. Bruner identified that learning is an active process in which learners construct new ideas or concepts based upon their current and past knowledge. The practitioner's role is to scaffold the child's learning by, for example, providing prompts, a little more knowledge, resources, and modelling skills. Therefore, Bruner advocated that the curriculum should be organised in a spiral manner so that children are continually able to re-visit experiences that they are interested in and build on the knowledge and learning that they already possess.

REFLECTION ACTIVITY 8.4

Consider how Floyd's key person used Bruner's theory of the spiral curriculum to help Floyd understand the process of growth.

How did Floyd's key person use her knowledge, observations and discussion with Floyd's mum to individualise the planning for his learning?

How did Floyd's key person scaffold his knowledge in a format that was appropriate for his age and stage of cognitive development?

How does this example of the experience offered to Floyd compare with how you plan for children's next steps in learning?

THE STAGES OF CHILD-CENTRED PLANNING

In planning for children aged 2 to 3 years you may wish to use the child-centred planning process illustrated in Chapter 7 and use long-term planning (LTP) as described to underpin the philosophy and ethos of the provision. For this age group, the medium-term planning (MTP) should be used to ensure that children are provided with a broad and balanced learning experience, encompassing all areas of learning and based on predictable events and experiences throughout the year.

MEDIUM-TERM PLANNING FOR CHILDREN AGED BETWEEN 2 AND 3 YEARS

In Chapter 7 we illustrated a medium-term plan for spring; here we present a medium term plan for autumn two and winter one (Table 8.1).

Table 8.1 Medium-term plan for autumn two and winter one

	Autumn 2 & Winter 1
What is the theme?	Autumn, colours, food, dark and light. Festivals, changes in the season, light and dark
When will it happen?	Autumn

Topics to be covered?	Changes in the season
	Red, yellow, orange, brown, white and green
	Festival foods
	Light and dark, shiny and dull
	Festivals:
	
	    Divali
	    Bonfire night
	    Christingle
	    Christmas/early winter
	    The advent
	    Chanukah
	    Eid
	
	Birds – migration, winter birds – feeding the birds
	Hibernation
	Light and dark:
	
	    Changes of season
	    Fireworks
	    Electricity
	
	Journeys – travel, geography, post

Schemas to be supported	Transportation

Learning possibilities	Autumn colours and shades
	What happens in autumn?
	Dark and light colours
	Metal and paper
	Diverse foods
	About different cultures and festivals
	Birds and flight and hibernation
	About fireworks and safety
	Simple circuits
	Sita and Rama
	Jesus
Special focus	UW
	EAD
	C & L
What concepts do we want the children to learn?	Texture
	Differences
	Colour
	Comparisons
	Sequence
	Capacity
	Environment
	Tradition
	Culture
	Distance
What skills do we want the children to develop?	Identifying
	Describing
	Connecting
	Observing
	Questioning
	Role playing
	Classifying
	Explaining
	Experimenting
What attitudes/ dispositions do we want the children to develop?	Absorbing
	Enthusiastic and persistent
	Positive
	Curious
	Being sensitive to the needs of others and living things
	Interested
	Patient
	Self-discipline and confidence
How will we address the children's different learning styles?	Musically – through songs
	Auditory
	Environment
	Kinesthetic
	Hands on experience collecting and exploring materials and nature
How will we involve parents in the theme and their children's learning?	Handouts for parents about the theme
How will we promote equal opportunities with this theme?	Use, smell and taste
	Festival foods
	Learn about Rama and Sita
How will we promote racial equality?	Positive images and staff knowledge of different festivals and cultures

(Continued)

Table 8.1 (Continued)

What do staff need in order to support the children's learning in this theme?	Children and adults in appropriate clothing Staff well informed about festivals
What teaching methods will be used to support the children's learning?	Asking questions Direct teaching Scaffolding Modelling Project work
How do we need to change the environment in order to support the children's learning?	Displays, interactive materials, autumnal collections – leaves, sticks, pine cones, conkers etc., lights, shiny, post office
How will we monitor and evaluate the effectiveness of the teaching and learning?	Observation and assessment Evaluate the medium term Discussion with parents Photographs
How will we plan the curriculum for individual children?	Through observations, assessments, discussions with parents, colleagues and children. Enhance the continuous provision to meet children's individual learning needs and interests and respond in the moment.
How will we assess the children's individual progress?	Observing children in play, written observations, evaluation of children's learning, up-to-date records and review with parents.
Key questions for assessment	What colour is it? What does it smell like? Which one is shiny? When and where is it dark? What is it like in the den? Where do you think the birds are flying? Which animals have a long sleep in the winter? What are the little diva lamps for? What do you need to make a cake? How many days until Christmas? What happens when you post a card? Who brings you presents? What happened at the bonfire? Tell me the story of the nativity

SHORT-TERM PLANNING FOR CHILDREN AGED BETWEEN 2 AND 3 YEARS

Short-term planning (STP) is where experiences are tailored to cater for the children's individual development, interests and learning needs. Mostly, this is likely to be planning in the moment by a key person responding to the interests, actions and interactions of their key children, as demonstrated in the longitudinal observation of Floyd. Sometimes, the short-term planning will also record how you provide resources and enhancements to the continuous provision in response to children's schematic play and interests, as illustrated in the case study of Samantha's setting. Within our short-term planning, the strongest link between assessment and planning is forged.

We develop our knowledge of each individual 2-year-old through our observations, discussions with parents, the children themselves and colleagues. We use what we know about children to plan experiences to support and extend their learning and development and also to be alert to the need to adapt our teaching in response to young children's ideas, interests and questions. This was illustrated in the observation of Floyd when the practitioner responded to her observations of him and supported his learning over time. The teaching was tailored to Floyd's particular learning needs in the moment. It is important to remember that in child-centred planning practitioners cannot possibly write everything down. We adapt our teaching in response to something that sparks a 2-year-old's particular interest. If we have built learning into the environment through our long-term and medium-term plans, the short-term plans will be tailored specifically to the individual learning and developmental needs of children aged 2 to 3 years.

CONCLUSION

In planning for 2- to 3-year-old children it is therefore important that we are responsive and flexible and understand that when something really interests the children their learning can be sustained over a number of months. Confidence and self-esteem are built as the 2-year-old works hard on something that is rewarding and they learn that being persistent leads to success. Therefore, it is important that 2-year-olds are provided with time and opportunities to consolidate their learning and build upon it, as recommended by Bruner's spiral curriculum. For 2-year-olds, becoming independent is fuelled by wanting to make things happen and building on their growing knowledge of how things have worked before. Two-year-olds will stand firm in their new-found independence – the word 'no' particularly with children who have just turned two years of age is frequently used – this is a good sign and is a declaration of independence. It is important that we allow them to develop pride in their competence and experience challenges, as finding their own way of doing things helps them to develop their knowledge, skills, successful attitudes to learning and gain more control over what happens to them. These are all essential if young children are to grow up to become independent and responsible adults.

In closing this chapter, we wish to remind you of the crucial role of the key person relationship with the 2-year-old and their family. It is especially important that children of this age, some of whom may also be vulnerable, have someone in the provision who 'sees' them and their family as special. It is incredibly important that this person is a consistent, trusted adult that reliably responds to the very individual and personal needs of the terrific 2-year-olds in their care.

FURTHER READING

Bruce, T (2011) *Learning through Play* (2nd edn). London: Hodder Education.

Georgeson, J, Campbell-Barr, V and TACTYC (Association for Professional Development in Early Years) (2018) *Places for Two-year-olds in the Early Years: Supporting Learning and Development*. London: Routledge.

Greenman, J, Stonehouse, A and Schweikert, G (2007) *Prime Times* (2nd edn). St Paul, MN: Redleaf Press.

Sheridan, M D (1975) *From Birth to Five Years: Children's Developmental Progress*. London: Routledge.

REFERENCES

Arnold, C and the Pen Green Team (2010) *Understanding Schemas and Emotion in Early Childhood*. London: Sage.

Athey, C (1991) *Extending Thought in Young Children's Learning: A Parent–Teacher Partnership*. London: Paul Chapman.

Bruner, J (1957) *Jerome Bruner's Theory of Development: Discovery Learning & Representation*. Available at https://study.com/academy/lesson/jerome-bruners-theory-of-development-discovery-learning-representation.html

Department for Education (2017) *The Statutory Framework for the Early Years Foundation Stage*. London: DfE.

Duncan, J and Lockwood, M (2008) *A Work-based Approach for the Early Years Professional*. London: Continuum International Publishing Group.

Early Education (2012) *Development Matters in the Early Years Foundation Stage (EYFS)*. London: Early Education. Available at https://www.foundationyears.org.uk/wp-content/uploads/2012/03/Development-Matters-FINAL-PRINT-AMENDED.pdf

Fisher, S and Revels, J (2014) *Tuning in to Two-year-olds: Improving Outcomes for Two-year-olds*. London: Harrow Council.

Isaacs, S (1933) *The Nursery Years: The Mind of the Child from Birth to Six Years*. London: Routledge & Kegan Paul.

Piaget, J (1957) *Construction of Reality in the Child*. London: Routledge & Kegan Paul.

Sharma, A and Cockerill, H (2014) *Mary Sheridan's From Birth to Five Years: Children's Developmental Progress*. Abingdon: Routledge.

Tassoni, P and Tassoni, A M (2018) *Follow Me: What Are the Developmental Expectations for Attention and Listening in Two-to-Three-year-olds and When Should Concerns be Raised?* London: Nursery World MA Education.

9 PLANNING FOR PRE-SCHOOLERS

FROM 36 TO 48 MONTHS

Jo McEvoy and Kate Smith

CHAPTER AIMS

By the end of this chapter you will be able to:

- describe how children aged 3–4 years learn
- start to plan a safe and stimulating environment that supports holistic learning
- consider how to respond to children's interests and plan spontaneously to meet the needs of individual children and groups of children
- consider ways to plan for phase one phonics using 'Letters and Sounds'

INTRODUCTION

Pre-school children are typically gaining in confidence and independence, exploring boundaries and presenting with a diverse and exciting range of interests, knowledge and skills. Children of this age are, by their very nature, inquisitive and curious. Yet, every 3- and 4-year-old child is different, so the journey of sharing and supporting their learning has the potential to be as unique as their individual development. This chapter will consider the learning and development needs of children in the pre-school year, taking account of the different types of Early Years Foundation Stage (EYFS) settings they attend. It will promote a holistic and spontaneous approach to planning, which recognises the vital role of the enabling environment in supporting children's well-being, learning and development.

As in the previous two chapters, we will begin by considering what we recognise as typical characteristics of 3- to 4-year-olds.

REFLECTION ACTIVITY 9.1

Think of a 3-year-old child that you know. What is he/she like? What are their interests? How does she/he behave and what can she/he do?

Think of words and sentences that describe your child.

Now compare your list with some of the developmental milestones listed in the 30–50 months bands of the prime areas of learning in the *Development Matters* guidance.

What do you notice about your list and the list of 'typical' development in the guidance? It is likely that there are differences between the two because no two children are the same and each of our pre-school children has their own unique funds of knowledge, interests and experiences.

THE PRE-SCHOOL YEAR

Children of 3 to 4 years of age are often referred to as pre-schoolers, as they are in the year prior to starting school in the Reception class. Most children of this age are attending some type of pre-school provision for at least 15 hours a week, as they take up their entitlement to government-funded Early Years education. They attend a variety of different types of EYFS provision, depending on the childcare needs and personal choices of their parents. Some attend pre-school settings that accommodate children from 2 to 5 years in one group, others attend a private day Nursery and are cared for as a small group of 3–4-year-olds in one room, while many will attend a Nursery class of 3–4-year-olds in a primary school. Historically, day care settings and pre-schools have operated in a predominantly social paradigm, while Nursery classes in schools have operated in a more academic paradigm. However, when the first statutory guidance for the EYFS was published in 2008, Early Years settings started to adopt a more holistic approach to the cycle of assessment, planning and teaching and the current EYFS (DfE, 2017) continues to promote this approach. Therefore, although the types of settings attended by this group of children may be different in how they operate, they are all required to plan holistically for learning, taking account of the individual needs of each unique child.

HOLISTIC LEARNING

Holistic learning encompasses a recognition of the unique child. It promotes the child's individual physical, personal, social, emotional and spiritual well-being, as well as their cognitive development. Practitioners promoting holistic learning recognise that children's learning is integrated and connected. They strive to build strong partnerships with parents so that they can gain a more authentic understanding of the child and also develop a shared approach to promoting their unique development. Adopting a holistic approach also requires practitioners to provide a highly stimulating learning environment, capable of inspiring inquiry-based learning, promoting independence and allowing a degree of risk taking. In the Reggio Emilia approach (Thornton and Brunton, 2005), this type of learning environment is known as 'the third teacher' because it has the capacity to provide pre-school children with a wealth of diverse learning opportunities tailored to their individual needs and interests. In the *Statutory Framework for the EYFS* this is described as the 'Enabling Environment' and is based on the principle that,

> *Children learn and develop well in enabling environments, in which their experiences respond to their individual needs and there is a strong partnership between practitioners and parents and/ or carers.*

(DfE, 2017, p6)

Within this chapter there are examples of what this looks like in practice. There are descriptions of how practitioners have 'tuned in' to children and adopted a holistic approach to support their development. They have embraced children's growing confidence and provided rich learning experiences that truly capture their curiosity and sense of wonder. To do this well, they have had to draw on their knowledge of how pre-school children learn and exercise professional judgement in making decisions about how best to support their development. The following explanations of how children learn provide you with guidance on how to apply your knowledge and professional judgement.

USING YOUR KNOWLEDGE AND PROFESSIONAL JUDGEMENT TO SUPPORT CHILDREN'S LEARNING

Vygotsky (1978) suggests that the zone of promixal development bridges the gap between what children currently know and what they have the potential to know. He proposes that this is the optimal time for learning and that scaffolding new ideas built around children's interests helps to support cognitive changes. He suggests that working collaboratively with a practitioner or with peers can help a child make progress in their learning.

Your role in planning for learning is to use your knowledge and exercise professional judgement by:

1. securely assessing what the child already knows and can do;
2. spotting the optimal time for learning by tuning into the child's interest;
3. knowing what to do next to extend the child's learning.

Ferre Laevers' (2005) research into children's well-being and their levels of involvement, which can be assessed using his Leuven scales of well-being and involvement, suggests that optimal learning takes place when children are emotionally secure and deeply involved. The important role of the child's key person in helping to support a secure attachment is pivotal in helping to promote a sense of belonging (Bowlby, 1953), and a key person will often use the Leuven scales to support their understanding of how comfortable and emotionally secure their child is feeling at the start of the day. Through this emotional security, children gain confidence to begin to explore their learning environment.

Your role in planning for learning is to use your knowledge and exercise professional judgement by:

1. knowing how to use and interpret the Leuven scales of well-being and involvement devised by Ferre Laevers;
2. forming a strong attachment with your key children and their families;
3. planning the environment in a way that motivates children to want to explore.

Yuhas (2014) cites the research of neuroscientist, Charan Ranganath (Gruber et al., 2014), who suggests that curiosity prepares the brain for learning and aids long-term memory. Being curious also helps to trigger parts of the brain that regulate pleasure and reward. As young children act on their curiosity, they engage in inquiry-based learning. A stimulating environment that captures their interest and enables children to have time to think and try out their ideas helps to support effective learning. Your role in planning for learning is to use your knowledge and exercise professional judgement by:

1. planning provocations to capture children's curiosity;
2. having courage to give children the time they need to become fully engrossed in play;
3. knowing how and when to intervene to support or extend children's thinking.

REFLECTION ACTIVITY 9.2

Consider the suggestions listed above that describe how you might use your knowledge and professional judgement when deciding on how best to plan for children's learning.

From these suggestions draw up a list of your strengths and areas for development.

Decide on one action you can take to support one of your areas for development.

TIME TO PLAY

Exploratory play promotes children's thinking and helps to foster their resilience as they try out their thoughts and ideas. A thoughtfully planned learning environment provides pre-school children with a wide range of indoor and outdoor resources available through continuous provision. These are available for children to explore through independent play or shared investigation with peers. Deep-level learning takes place when children have the opportunity to play for sustained periods of time (Moyles, 2012). It is essential therefore that children have time to develop the complexity of their play (Wood, 2013). Pre-school children are bursting with creative ideas, a flurry of language and the confidence to try things out. They need opportunities to develop creative thought and critical problem-solving skills as these are life skills that will aid them and society in the future. However, often the daily routine of a pre-school class/setting does not enable children to engage in deep levels of play for sustained periods of time to help maximise their thinking skills. There are often frequent interruptions to children's play as they are called to the carpet for circle time, phonics, story, snacks and other activities. Reflective practitioners however, are able to utilise their knowledge and professional judgement to effect positive changes.

CASE STUDY 9.1

Sarah Collins, Early Years Teacher (EYT)

Our pre-school routine involved lots of carpet time sessions and a sit down snack time. Although the snack routine was planned with a purpose in mind – to promote PSED and communication and language through sitting in key groups with our children, it took up a lot of time. Children were having to stop and tidy up for snack time and this interrupted their child-initiated play. I was training to be an EYT at the time and I became interested in learning about sustained shared thinking and developing children's thinking skills. After research and reflection I decided to implement a snack café in the continuous provision, a rolling snack time to enable a more flexible approach. It was not an easy option because I had to convince the rest of the staff to give it a go and this meant me knowing my subject well and being able to explain my professional judgement to more experienced staff. However, they were happy to support me and we gave it a go. The results were amazing. The snack café was successful and had a very positive impact, enabling children to choose when to leave their play. As a result, children were able to play without unnecessary interruptions and we were better placed to be able to become involved in children's play, scaffolding their thinking through sensitive questions, prompts and challenges.

REFLECTION ACTIVITY 9.3

Why do you think children need sustained periods of time to engage in exploratory play?

Develop your knowledge of how pre-school children learn, by finding out about 'Sustained Shared Thinking' and how you might provide opportunities for this in your planning (see reference list – try Kathy Brodie's book, *Sustained Shared Thinking in the Early Years*).

PLANNING FOR PRE-SCHOOL CHILDREN

HOW DO WE KNOW WHAT CHILDREN ALREADY KNOW AND CAN DO?

Hearing and respecting the voice of the child is essential to capturing their unique qualities. There are many ways that children can express their thoughts and ideas, for example through words, actions and art. In previous chapters of the book, the use of observation has been readily discussed to ascertain children's current interests and their stage of development. In a pre-school room, a baseline assessment for starting points for learning will often include the prime areas and the specific areas of learning within the EYFS. As discussed in Chapter 8, parents' contribution to this helps to give a more 'rounded' view of what children can confidently do in their home learning environments. Some settings are highly skilled at establishing strong partnership working prior to children starting to attend. This helps to maximise their transition into the setting.

✓   TIPS FOR PRACTICE: READY, STEADY, NURSERY!

Emma Turner, Nursery class teacher established a series of 'Ready, Steady, Nursery' stay and play sessions for parents and children. These take place during the term prior to children starting to attend her Nursery class. Activities such as story-telling with props, manipulating dough, promoting self-help skills, fostering social skills and a taster Forest School session help to establish shared experiences. These contribute to building on-going relationships with children and parents, fostering a collaborative approach to supporting children's development. Effective home learning links help to support a holistic approach and continuity for children. Through effective use of observation and strong partnership working, starting points for children's learning can clearly be established during the first weeks of attendance. This enables practitioners to plan tailored next steps for children's individual learning. These are built around their interest and contribute to progressing their learning and quickly closing potential gaps in their development.

BUILDING ON WHAT CHILDREN KNOW AND CAN DO

The Statutory Framework for the EYFS informs practitioners that they must,

consider the individual needs, interests, and stage of development of each child in their care, and must use this information to plan a challenging and enjoyable experience for each child in all of the areas of learning and development.

(DfE, 2017, p9)

There is no right or wrong way to plan. Every setting will adopt an approach that works for them and their children. Often practitioners will reflect on whether their planning is 'meaningful and useful' or too long-winded and bureaucratic. As detailed in Chapter 1, planning can take the form of long term, medium term and short term.

LONG-TERM PLANNING

Examples of long-term planning for a pre-school class or a school Nursery class will include the creation of an inclusive, safe and stimulating indoor and outdoor learning environment. This takes the form of continuous provision. Since pre-school children are becoming more confident in their gross motor skills they are more likely to want to be outside so the outdoor learning environment requires careful planning. Outdoor experiences often include opportunities for children to maximise their gross motor skills, try out their ideas on a bigger scale and take appropriate risks in their play.

✓   TIPS FOR PRACTICE: LOOSE PARTS PLAY

- consists of offering children a variety of collections of everyday objects, materials and natural resources
- easy to resource and set up
- enables children to move and combine a range of open-ended resources in a variety of different ways
- helps to foster innovative thought and creativity
- prepares children for their future learning by teaching them to be original as well as competent

(Csikszentmihalyi, 1997)

Figure 9.1   Examples of loose parts play

MEDIUM-TERM PLANNING

Medium-term planning incorporates children's interests and may develop a certain theme to reflect their ideas and thoughts. For example, young children often develop an interest in dinosaurs or pirates. The planning over a number of weeks, until children's interest wanes, will incorporate opportunities to build on this, supporting all areas of learning. In the example plan (Table 9.1) the practitioners simply plan suggested activities and experiences that their children may find interesting. They do not list the learning objectives, since they recognise that these will be different for every child and are addressed through the short-term planning. The children are in key person groups and the key person uses the cycle of 'observe, assess and plan' (Early Education, 2012) for each key child in their short-term planning. Thus, the room is set up with activities from the medium-term plan, but the key person is responsible for observing their key children, assessing their development and responding to their learning needs through their interactions or providing more challenge or different experiences.

Table 9.1 Example medium-term plan for pre-school room

Physical development	PSED	Communication + Language
• Dinosaur bone hunt – archaeological dig in the garden • Egg hunt – quietly tiptoeing • Different dinosaur movements, e.g. stomping, flying, tiptoeing, swimming • Malleable area – making dinosaur eggs and bones • Dinosaur foot path – moving bodies in different ways to follow dinosaur path • Dinosaur tail chase – carnivore chasing herbivores	• Exploring emotions of the dinosaurs: • Before meteorite – living in family groups, hunting for prey • During darkness – lack of food etc. • Different personalities of dinosaurs – gentle and kind, fierce and frightening • Who is your favourite dinosaur? Examine reasoning • Dinosaur who travels to children's houses with book and props	• Introduction to dinosaur terminology – meteorite, lava, ash, darkness • More advanced: omnivore, herbivore, carnivore. Also the periods: jurassic, metazoic, triassic, cretaceous • 'Millions (65) of years ago' … understanding of what this means? • Family grouping discussions around dinosaurs to encourage conversation, listening, turn taking and role modelling

DINOSAURS			

Literacy	Mathematics	Expressive Arts & Design	Understanding the World
• Clipboards to write down the 'excavation notes' child led • Dinosaur stories – 'Dinosaur Roar', 'I Dreamt I Was a Dinosaur', 'Dinosaurs Love Underpants'. • Drawing of dinosaur feet – making a 'Dino Trail' independently/ with support for friends to use • Turn book area into dinosaur nest	• Comparison of dinosaur sizes – measure with stick/ string and mark out on the floor for idea of scale • Grouping & sorting re: type, size, colour, which era – • Ordering • Counting • Estimation – dinosaur steps to child's steps	• Papier-mâché volcanoes • Creating meteors • Footprints • Junk 3D dinosaur feet, wings, heads • Describing, designing and creating large scale dinosaurs • Outdoor 3D nests – dino eggs to be incubated and hatched	• Dropping meteors from decking – understanding 'crashing to earth'/gravity • Bicarb of soda and vinegar in volcanoes – lava and eruption – extinction of species • 'Big Bang Theory' – See above. • Descendants of dinosaurs today • Tablets – 'watch' dino movement – how & why

Medium-term plan created by Rainbows Nursery, Salford

SHORT-TERM PLANNING

The Statutory Framework for the EYFS states that,

> *in their interactions with children, practitioners should respond to their own day-to-day observations about children's progress and observations that parents and carers share.*

(DfE, 2017, p13)

This, in essence, is short-term planning. Short-term planning is where you are able to respond in the exact moment when you spot a learning opportunity and to build in 'next steps' to help consolidate and extend children's individual development. Practitioners plan for children's next steps in learning and carry them out in a variety of ways, for example, with one child or with a small group. Children in pre-school or school Nursery classes learn through social interaction with their peers. Practitioners can 'instruct' through adult-led activities, or 'guide' through child-initiated activities. However, as Early Years learning is rooted in rich play opportunities, practitioners will also seek opportunities to weave children's individual next steps into their play. They build on their current interests and maintain their motivation and enthusiasm for learning in different ways; for example, by modelling new skills and knowledge, talking about what is happening and engaging children in sustained shared thinking. The following case study illustrates all of these approaches.

CASE STUDY 9.2

Aeroplane play

Starting point – Bob has relatives that live in Ireland and he often visits them at weekends. Spending lots of time at the airport has created a big interest in aeroplanes.

Activity – While building in the construction area, Bob started talking to an adult about the big blue aeroplane that he went on at the weekend. 'Let's make an aeroplane', he said. The adult encouraged Bob to talk about the different parts that he noticed on the aeroplane, e.g. chairs, wings, wheels etc. and then together they looked for objects that they could use to create their own aeroplane. By this time a small group of children had also shown interest and joined in the play.

Together the group began constructing the aeroplane with the adult modelling lots of mathematical language relating to size and shape. When finished, the group then initiated a role-play scenario with Bob being the pilot and the rest of the group being the passengers. The adult modelled new vocabulary, such as 'pilot', 'luggage', runway' and provided paper and pens for the children to make their own tickets and passports. The children each had a turn at being the pilot and decided where the aeroplane was going to fly to next. They visited the beach, Ireland, Disneyland, Asda and various other places. The children were keen to share their stories and talk about places they had visited with their family.

Following on from this we asked parents/carers to send in photographs of their children visiting different places and displayed them in the room. This was a fantastic way to get the children to talk about themselves and the things they do outside of Nursery. Staff found that this was particularly effective with the children who were often quite shy and quiet during group discussion.

Case study created by Rainbows Nursery, Salford

In this example of planning in the moment, the practitioner drew on her knowledge of the child to understand that he had a wealth of experience of aeroplanes to inform his play. She tuned into his interest and supported him and all the children to gain new knowledge, extend their vocabulary, develop their mark-making skills and their imagination. Bob was able to lead the play which would boost his confidence and self-esteem, but other children too made significant progress in joining in group discussions for the first time. This type of planning was not written down in advance, nor were the learning objectives pre-planned. The knowledgeable practitioner was able to exercise professional judgement in deciding how to scaffold the learning, extend knowledge and model skills.

It really is very wonderful when you start to see the difference that planning in a child-centred way makes, not only to children's learning, but also to your own practice and professional confidence. Sarah Collins was training to be an EYT when she learned about child-centred planning and responding to children's learning in the moment (see Case study 9.3). She described it as her 'light bulb moment', the day when she responded spontaneously to a child's interest and had amazing results in terms of the children's engagement, motivation and learning. From then on she made the decision to move away from planning weekly activities in advance for groups of children and now concentrates on tuning in to children's interests, planning in the moment and responding to their individual learning and developmental needs.

CASE STUDY 9.3

The bear hunt

These are Sarah's notes with some pictures from the book she made for the children to re-visit the story of their very own bear hunt.

Sitting down at lunchtime asking the children about what they did at the weekend. Child mentioned that they went on a bear hunt so we decided to go on one too.

I suggested we needed to write down a list of all the things we might need so I got a large whiteboard and a pen. The children shared their ideas and I scribed the list on the board for them.

The children wanted to draw some maps so we collected some paper and mark-making resources.

The children then drew other things too, a lunchbox, footprints and a bear.

We planned our bear hunt, packed our bags and collected our binoculars.

As we set off on our walk the children told aspects of the story, 'Swishy, swashy grass'.

We were fortunate to have a very large cuddly bear at the setting and it had been placed on the field behind the setting.

The children spotted the bear and ran towards it. One of the children wanted to take a photo of it on the camera.

The children wanted the bear to play on the park.

They worked together to move him around the play equipment.

The next day, back in the setting, one child found the big book of the bear hunt and wanted to read it. She was able to point to the words left to right as an adult read her the story.

(Continued)

(Continued)

The children wanted to make mud. A sensory tray was made. Staff and children sourced various resources to relate to the story – grass, rock, water, mud. The children retold the story as they played with it.

A member of staff accidently made a catapult with a spoon by leaning on it. The compare bears had been introduced to the sensory tray by the children so they started to catapult the bears. Children worked out independently how to balance the spoon on the rock at the correct angle to make the catapult work effectively. Soon there were bears flying everywhere!

Sarah was struck by how much more the children learned through responding immediately to their interests and making good use of the learning environment. It was the children who set up the sensory tray with some adult support, the children who re-enacted the story and it was the children who became interested in the cata-pulting game, which continued for several days. They were not just learning about literacy through the story. Their learning was holistic, covering many different skills and aspects of knowledge.

REFLECTION ACTIVITY 9.4

Read through the case study again. Can you list the skills and knowledge that children were gaining through this experience?

Have you had or observed similar opportunities in your setting where you might have responded immediately to children's interests?

DAILY PLANNING FOR PHASE ONE LETTERS AND SOUNDS

Teaching phonics as part of early reading is now well established in our schools and Nursery classes. Since the Rose review in 2006, synthetic phonics has been introduced as the preferred method for teaching phonics in schools. There is still a deep running debate about the place of phonics in early reading and especially in the pre-school year of education. The crucial point in this debate is not whether phonics is the right way to teach reading, but whether children are developmentally ready to learn phonics. The guidance document *Letters and Sounds* (DfE, 2007) sets out a structured route to be followed in teaching phonics and the foundation of that route is phase one, 'tuning into sound'. It really can-not be emphasised strongly enough how important this phase is in paving the way for children to make great progress in their future development in reading. If children are secure in phase one, then they are able to:

- differentiate between the subtle differences in sounds leading to recognising sounds (phonemes) that make up words for reading and writing;

- recognise syllables in words, which helps with spelling;
- hear and say the initial sounds in words, which gives them a clue as to what the word might be;
- recognise similar patterns in words that rhyme or are associated through alliteration;
- be confident to articulate clearly the sounds in words that they hear;
- blend phonemes together for reading and segment sounds for spelling.

All of these steps are the foundations for being able to read and write words. They support word recognition skills, needed to become a competent reader, but they are not the only skills and attributes required for learning to read. Children also need good comprehension skills and knowledge of books and how stories are structured. They need imagination, vocabulary, confidence and motivation. There are many different elements to be taken into account when teaching reading, and phonics is just one of them, but a vital one that needs you to teach it in a developmentally appropriate way, particularly in the pre-school year. Many pre-school classes choose to plan for phonics in a structured way on a daily basis. The template in Table 9.2 is an example of how you might record your planning for phase one. However, all of the seven aspects of phase one in *Letters and Sounds* (DfE, 2007) are skills that young children can develop through their everyday play experiences throughout the pre-school year, if they are taught by knowledgeable adults.

In Rainbows Nursery the staff view the teaching of phase one phonics as part of their daily teaching through continuous provision.

CASE STUDY 9.4

Phase one phonics: small groups and everywhere

Letters and sounds is not really something that we have a specific time for during the Nursery day but something that is embedded into our activities and everyday routines. An example of this would be when our 3-year-olds went out on their autumn walk to collect natural objects, we took the time to listen to what was going on around us as we walked. … leaves underfoot, cars driving past and birds in the trees. Children are really encouraged to explore the sounds they can make with natural and man-made objects inside and outside and using their own bodies too during action rhymes and songs. Music plays a big part in our day and children sing and listen to music and can operate our CD player to play songs or use tablets to record and play back their own voices. In the playroom we have a 'magic box' that contains all sorts of items which can be used to support the different aspects of phase one phonics. For example, there are items that are useful for making noises to support children's sound discrimination skills. Other items are used by adults to model segmenting, for example, by sounding out the phonemes that make up a word and the children guess what it is.

Case study by Rainbows Nursery, Salford

Table 9.2   Planning template for phase one phonics

Age range	Key learning intention	Links to EYFS
3–4 years	To distinguish between different sounds (Phase one general sound discrimination, musical instruments)	To develop listening and attention skills
Activity	Play Grandmother's footsteps from Letters and Sounds	
Adult directed	Model how Grandmother moves forward matching the musical instrument, e.g. triangle = tiny tiptoes, drum = large strides etc. Children practise moving round the room matching movements as modelled by the teacher. Hide the instruments from sight and repeat Play game where Grandmother stands with her back to the others and plays an instrument. The other children move towards Grandmother in the manner of the instrument while it is playing. They stop when it stops. The first person to reach Grandmother takes over that role and the game starts again	
Opportunity for child initiated learning	Provide a box of musical instruments outside and dressing up clothes for Grandmother, for children to play the game independently	
	Provide a box of objects for children to make up their own sounds and movements to play the game	
	Leave different 'beaters', e.g. dowelling, spoons attached to the fence and metal railings for children to explore the different sounds they can make	
	Provide resources for children to make own musical instruments in the workshop area	
Resources	Box of musical instruments: tambourine, maraca, castanets, drum, triangle, bells, rainmaker Workshop resources for making own musical instruments Spoons, sticks, dowelling, plastic spades for attaching to fences	
Look, Listen, Note	Children who can match movement to the musical instruments (memory, listening, concentrating) Children who are eager to join in (CoEL) Children who may mix up similar sounds (rainmaker, maraca) Children willing to explore and experiment (CoEL) Children who start to use the instruments or resources to tap out a rhythm	
Evaluation		

CONCLUSION

This chapter has discussed how pre-school children typically learn and has established that children of this age are naturally curious, imaginative and becoming much more confident in developing and using their physical and language skills. It has promoted a holistic approach to planning that follows children's immediate interests and makes optimal use of the physical learning environment. It has highlighted the need for you to be flexible in your approach to foster individual learning. Often this necessitates being an observer, a facilitator or a participator.

Your planning is an essential tool to enable you to do this well. It can be proactive or reactive to best meet children's needs. Holistic planning is nurturing, flexible and adaptable. It enables you to respond to 'the here and now' and build in future learning opportunities. The chapter identified that a wealth of learning experiences can be child-initiated. Therefore, planning a safe and stimulating environment to capture children's interests and curiosity is essential to spark their interest in learning. Enhancing the environment in response to their interests and modelling new skills and knowledge will then help to further extend and consolidate children's development. Children's need for sustained periods of time to become engrossed in play has also been raised as particularly important for this age group, as it supports the development of their thinking skills and provides opportunities for children and adults to engage together in sustained shared thinking. Phase one phonics has been discussed as one aspect of developing early reading skills and examples of how this phase can be embedded in everyday practice have been illustrated. Above all, this chapter has highlighted that your role in planning for the pre-school year is to get to know your children well through observational assessment and finding out about their backgrounds and families. This will enable you to establish their strengths and learning needs and then to plan open-ended playful experiences that will appeal to their curiosity and motivate them to want to explore and develop their knowledge, understanding and skills. The pre-school year is a very exciting one in terms of children's growing independence, confidence and inquisitiveness. It is hoped that you will treasure the fun and satisfaction you get as a practitioner planning for their unique learning journeys in the unique type of setting where you work, or learn through your placement.

FURTHER READING

Bottrill, G (2018) *Can I Go and Play Now?* London: Sage.
Daly, L and Beloglovsky, M (2014) *Loose Parts: Inspiring Play in Young Children.* St Paul, MN: Redleaf Press.
Neaum, S (2017) *What Comes Before Phonics.* London. Sage/Learning Matters.

REFERENCES

Bowlby, J (1953) *Child Care and the Growth of Love.* London: Penguin Books.
Brodie, K (2014) *Sustained Shared Thinking in the Early Years: Linking Theory to Practice.* London: Routledge.
Csikszentmihalyi, M (1979) The concept of flow, in Sutton-Smith, B (ed), *Play and Learning* (pp257–73). New York: Gardner.
Department for Children, Schools and Families (DCSF) (2008) *Statutory Framework for the Early Years Foundation Stage.* Nottingham: DCSF.
Department for Education (2007) *Letters and Sounds.* Available at www.gov.uk/government/publications/letters-and-sounds
Department for Education (2017) *The Statutory Framework for the Early Years Foundation Stage.* London: DfE.
Early Education (2012) *Development Matters in the Early Years Foundation Stage (EYFS).* London: Early Education. Available at https://www.foundationyears.org.uk/wp-content/uploads/2012/03/Development-Matters-FINAL-PRINT-AMENDED.pdf
Gruber, M J, Gelman, B D and Ranganath, C (2014) States of curiosity modulate hippocampus-dependent learning via the dopaminergic circuit. *Neuron, 84*: 486–96, cited in Yuhas, D (2014) *Curiosity Prepares the Brain for Better Learning.* Available at www.scientificamerican.com/article/curiosity-prepares-the-brain-for-better-learning/ (accessed 6 October 2018).

Laevers, F (2005) *Deep-level-learning and the Experiential Approach in Early Childhood and Primary Education*. Available at https://vorming.cego.be/images/downloads/BO_DP_Deep-levelLearning.pdf (accessed 8 October 2018).

Moyles, J (2012) *A to Z of Play in Early Childhood*. Maidenhead: Open University Press.

Rose, J (2006) *Independent Review of the Teaching of Early Reading*. Available at http://dera.ioe.ac.uk/5551/2/report.pdf

Thornton, L and Brunton, P (2005) *Understanding the Reggio Approach*. London: David Fulton Publishers.

Vygotsky, L S (1978) *Mind in Society: The Development of Higher Psychological Processes*. Cambridge, MA: Harvard University Press.

Wood, E (2013) *Play, Learning and the Early Childhood Curriculum* (3rd edn). London: Sage.

Yuhas, D (2014) *Curiosity Prepares the Brain for Better Learning*. Available at www.scientificamerican.com/article/curiosity-prepares-the-brain-for-better-learning/ (accessed 6 October 2018).

10 PLANNING FOR THE RECEPTION CLASS

Jo McEvoy

CHAPTER AIMS

By the end of this chapter you will be able to:

- understand the learning and development needs of children aged 4–5 years
- discuss the challenges that may be associated with planning for children in the Reception class
- consider different approaches to Reception class planning
- develop your own rationale for planning in the Reception class

INTRODUCTION

Planning for child-centred learning in the Reception class is often viewed as being problematic. Although it should not be the case, Reception class planning is notoriously challenging due to the influence of ambiguous messages about what and how children should be taught in this year group. The main difficulty lies in the fact that these children are still part of the Early Years Foundation Stage (EYFS), but are also part of a primary school. Thus, Reception class teaching is influenced by two contrasting pedagogical approaches.

On the one hand, the EYFS (DfE, 2017) promotes play-based learning within enabling environments that support children to develop positive dispositions to learning, as described in the Characteristics of Effective Learning (p10). The principles of the EYFS infer that teachers should plan holistically across all areas of learning, in partnership with parents and other professionals, to provide an enabling learning environment and a child-centred curriculum that responds to children's individual needs.

On the other hand, the National Primary Curriculum is predominantly knowledge-based and outcomes-focused. It is taught discretely through separate subjects (core and foundation subjects) with some opportunities for holistic planning across the foundation subjects and RE. Due to the age range of the children in this phase of education and the curriculum content, a more formal approach to teaching is adopted and children's learning is predominantly teacher-directed and teacher-guided.

A further complication that influences Reception class pedagogy and thus, the Reception class teacher's planning is that there appears to be a disparity in the EYFS itself, between its promotion of a child-centred pedagogy and its focus on outcomes, the Early Learning Goals (ELGs). The statutory framework for the Early

Years Foundation Stage (DfE, 2017) presents a view of the child as being 'Unique'. It states that children learn and develop at different rates and in different ways, yet it also outlines one set of universal goals that most children are expected to achieve by the end of the Reception year. Furthermore, it states that its purpose is to promote 'teaching and learning to ensure children's "school readiness"' (DfE, 2017, p5).

As a consequence of this emphasis on 'school readiness' and accountability, Early Years teachers have reported that they feel pressured to teach in more formal ways, planning more teacher-directed activities and more frequently using didactic methods for teaching (Roberts-Holmes, 2015). The impact of these pressures has also been reported in a study of Early Years teachers' pedagogical practices, in which Murray (2015) noted a dissonance between Early Years teachers' pedagogical values and their actual classroom practice. Thus, despite being in favour of a child-centred pedagogy, many Early Years teachers did not necessarily practise these approaches to planning and teaching in their classrooms.

It is not surprising, then, that Reception class teachers sometimes struggle to know how best to plan, to ensure that children are adequately prepared for the demands of the National Curriculum in year one, while also trying to adhere to the principles of the EYFS and its associated pedagogical practices.

Therefore, this chapter will support you to reflect on these challenges and begin to form your own opinions, based on your professional judgement and knowledge. It will discuss the dynamics of the Reception year with a focus on the end of year attainment outcomes. It will consider how children of this age typically learn and provide you with some examples of planning to stimulate ideas of how you might develop your practice.

THE RECEPTION YEAR

When children start in the Reception class they bring with them their own unique family and cultural experiences. They have very different starting points because each child already has a wealth of knowledge, skills and competencies drawn from their home life, the childcare settings they have attended and from the wider circles in which they live. Bronfenbrenner's (1979) ecological model of children's learning and development (explained in Chapter 2) illustrates this well.

On entering the school system in the Reception class, some children will already have experienced up to four years of group childcare, whilst others may not have accessed any childcare beyond their immediate families. Some are good communicators with a wide and varied vocabulary but others arrive with 'impoverished' speech and language (Communication Council, 2015), often leading to communication and social difficulties. Some will speak English as their home language, while others may find themselves in an English-speaking environment for the first time in their lives.

Some of these children who are learning English as a second language will be competent in their home language, but this may go unnoticed as they are unable to demonstrate their skills in a context where everyone is speaking in English. Similarly, some children may enter Reception with special educational needs or disabilities (SEND). They will, no doubt, have developed tremendously innovative and unique ways of coping and learning, but these too may go unnoticed if the context for learning is unfamiliar and barriers prevent them from demonstrating their capabilities. Likewise, for all the unique skills and competencies that children bring to the Reception class, if the context for learning is too rigid, it does not allow for children to show us their true capabilities and potential. Therefore, for the Reception class teacher it is all the more important that planning is child-centred, so that it capitalises on the wealth of experiences that children already have and builds on their prior learning to ensure that they can make the best progress possible.

REFLECTION ACTIVITY 10.1

What do you remember about your first year in school in the Reception class?

Were there any barriers for you that perhaps you were not aware of at the time, but you now can identify as an adult?

Looking back, do you think your teacher's planning was balanced more towards being child-centred or outcomes focused?

Regardless of the pedagogical stance they choose to adopt, Reception class teachers are all accountable for assessing children's achievements, identifying their learning needs and planning their provision to enable them to make progress towards achieving the end of EYFS outcomes, the Early Learning Goals (DfE, 2017).

EARLY LEARNING GOALS

The Early Learning Goals (ELGs) are outcomes. They describe the skills, knowledge and understanding that all children should achieve by the end of the Reception year (see Table 10.2 on pages 135–7 for the content of each ELG). There are 17 ELGs, one for each aspect of the seven areas of learning and development. Reception class teachers keep a focus on the ELGs throughout the year as they plan for learning. They are continually observing children to see if they are demonstrating the knowledge, skills and understanding outlined in each of the ELGs. In the summer term the class teacher summarises the children's attainment against the ELGs by stating if they are:

Emerging – the child is not yet achieving the ELG
Expected – the child has achieved the ELG
Exceeding – the child has achieved above the expectations for the ELG

The EYFS statutory guidance (DfE, 2017) requires all Reception class teachers to submit their outcomes data, known as the EYFS profile, to the local authority (LA) in the summer term and to report the children's attainment to their parents and Year 1 teachers. They are also required to write a brief commentary on the child's skills and abilities in relation to the three key characteristics of effective learning, but this is not reported to the LA, just to the parents and the Year 1 teacher. The LA must report these EYFS outcomes to the Department for Education (DfE).

THE GOOD LEVEL OF DEVELOPMENT

Success is measured by the number of children reaching the Good Level of Development (GLD). The GLD is deemed to be achieved if the child is expected to exceed in all of the ELGs within the following areas of learning:

- Personal, social and emotional development (PSED);
- Communication and language (C+L);
- Physical development (PD);
- Literacy (L);
- Mathematics (M).

Therefore, there are 12 ELGs that make up the GLD, as illustrated in Table 10.1.

Table 10.1 The 12 ELGs that make up the Good Level of Development (GLD)

Area of learning	Aspects	No. of ELGs
PSED	Making relationships	3
	Self-confidence and self-awareness	
	Managing feelings and behaviour	
Physical development	Moving and handling	3
	Health and self-care	
Communication and language	Listening and attention	2
	Understanding	
	Speaking	
Literacy	Reading	2
	Writing	
Mathematics	Numbers	2
	Shape, space and measure	

Targets

Primary schools will usually set targets for the percentage of children who are to achieve the GLD. This is likely to impact significantly on how Reception class teachers plan for children's learning. Having a target in place for a certain percentage of children to reach the GLD may result in teachers planning for outcomes, i.e. teaching to the assessment criteria, rather than planning for the particular needs of individual children, taking account of the smaller steps needed in order to achieve the long-term goal. Usually, this involves formal teaching strategies such as rote learning, direct teaching and instruction, which are likely to result in short-term gains. However, McDowell Clark (2017) argues against an earlier start to formal teaching in the Reception class. She cites the research findings of McClelland and Wanless (2015) which suggest that 'long term well-being and success at school are best supported by development of executive functioning and self-regulation abilities alongside satisfaction of children's need for feelings of autonomy, competence and relatedness' (McDowall Clark, 2017, p46).

These attributes are reminiscent of the Characteristics of Effective Learning (DfE, 2017, p10), highlighting the benefits to children of child-centred planning that prioritises children's dispositions to learning above a prescriptive set of outcomes. The following case study illustrates how focusing too much on the GLD in isolation can detract from child-centred planning and have negative consequences for Reception class children.

CASE STUDY 10.1

Janine (pseudonym), Reception class teacher

For two consecutive years we had mainly boys in our Reception class and many of them did not reach the ELG for writing. This meant that they therefore did not achieve the GLD and our EYFS profile results were below the LA average. Because of this, our senior leadership team requested that we gave children less time in continuous provision and planned daily writing and phonics activities into our weekly plans. We had children in guided reading and writing groups, intervention pencil control groups and daily sentence writing. Although more children managed to achieve the ELG for writing that year, there was a marked decline in the attention and engagement levels of the children, more problems with behaviour and we struggled to know who had achieved the ELG for Expressive Arts and Design, because we had less time and opportunities for children to demonstrate these skills. When it came to writing a summary of the child's Characteristics of Effective Learning I found it difficult because all of my interactions with the children were when I was sitting at tables doing directed teaching activities with them, or providing input on the carpet. It's difficult because, yes, we want all our children to reach the GLD and especially to be good readers and writers, but I do wonder if we are doing our children an injustice in planning so rigidly for the GLD and missing what they can do in other areas and building on what they have already achieved.

REFLECTION ACTIVITY 10.2

What do you think about the GLD being used as a measure of children being ready for school (the start of national curriculum in Year 1)?

List the skills, knowledge and attributes that you think are important for children to be well prepared for learning in Year 1.

Read through the 12 ELGs that make up the GLD (see Table 10.1, Table 10.2).

Is there anything on your list that is not contained within these 12 ELGs that make up the GLD?

Can you identify from your list any of the Characteristics of Effective Learning described in *Development Matters* pages 6–7?

Table 10.2 The Early Learning Goals (DfE, 2017, pp10–12)

Communication and language
• **Listening and attention:** children listen attentively in a range of situations. They listen to stories, accurately anticipating key events and respond to what they hear with relevant comments, questions or actions. They give their attention to what others say and respond appropriately, while engaged in another activity. • **Understanding:** children follow instructions involving several ideas or actions. They answer 'how' and 'why' questions about their experiences and in response to stories or events. • **Speaking:** children express themselves effectively, showing awareness of listeners' needs. They use past, present and future forms accurately when talking about events that have happened or are to happen in the future. They develop their own narratives and explanations by connecting ideas or events.

(Continued)

Table 10.2   (Continued)

Physical development

- **Moving and handling:** children show good control and co-ordination in large and small movements. They move confidently in a range of ways, safely negotiating space. They handle equipment and tools effectively, including pencils for writing.
- **Health and self-care:** children know the importance for good health of physical exercise, and a healthy diet, and talk about ways to keep healthy and safe. They manage their own basic hygiene and personal needs successfully, including dressing and going to the toilet independently.

Personal, social and emotional development

- **Self-confidence and self-awareness:** children are confident to try new activities, and say why they like some activities more than others. They are confident to speak in a familiar group, will talk about their ideas, and will choose the resources they need for their chosen activities. They say when they do or don't need help.
- **Managing feelings and behaviour:** children talk about how they and others show feelings, talk about their own and others' behaviour, and its consequences, and know that some behaviour is unacceptable. They work as part of a group or class, and understand and follow the rules. They adjust their behaviour to different situations, and take changes of routine in their stride.
- **Making relationships:** children play co-operatively, taking turns with others. They take account of one another's ideas about how to organise their activity. They show sensitivity to others' needs and feelings, and form positive relationships with adults and other children.

Literacy

- **Reading:** children read and understand simple sentences. They use phonic knowledge to decode regular words and read them aloud accurately. They also read some common irregular words. They demonstrate understanding when talking with others about what they have read.
- **Writing:** children use their phonic knowledge to write words in ways which match their spoken sounds. They also write some irregular common words. They write simple sentences which can be read by themselves and others. Some words are spelt correctly and others are phonetically plausible.

Mathematics

- **Numbers:** children count reliably with numbers from 1 to 20, place them in order and say which number is one more or one less than a given number. Using quantities and objects, they add and subtract two single-digit numbers and count on or back to find the answer. They solve problems, including doubling, halving and sharing.
- **Shape, space and measures:** children use everyday language to talk about size, weight, capacity, position, distance, time and money to compare quantities and objects and to solve problems. They recognise, create and describe patterns. They explore characteristics of everyday objects and shapes and use mathematical language to describe them.

Understanding the world

- **People and communities:** children talk about past and present events in their own lives and in the lives of family members. They know that other children don't always enjoy the same things, and are sensitive to this. They know about similarities and differences between themselves and others, and among families, communities and traditions.

- **The world:** children know about similarities and differences in relation to places, objects, materials and living things. They talk about the features of their own immediate environment and how environments might vary from one another. They make observations of animals and plants and explain why some things occur, and talk about changes.
- **Technology:** children recognise that a range of technology is used in places such as homes and schools. They select and use technology for particular purposes.

Expressive arts and design

- **Exploring and using media and materials:** children sing songs, make music and dance, and experiment with ways of changing them. They safely use and explore a variety of materials, tools and techniques, experimenting with colour, design, texture, form and function.
- **Being imaginative:** children use what they have learnt about media and materials in original ways, thinking about uses and purposes. They represent their own ideas, thoughts and feelings through design and technology, art, music, dance, role-play and stories.

PLANNING FOR THE RECEPTION CLASS

A good starting point for developing your approach to planning in Reception is for you to think about the following questions:

1. How do 4- and 5-year-olds typically learn? (This will inform how you plan for learning)
2. What does the EYFS statutory framework (DfE, 2017) require of me when I am planning? (This will inform how you plan for teaching)

LEARNING: HOW DO 4- AND 5-YEAR-OLDS LEARN?

Four and 5-year-olds are developing greater independence and autonomy. They typically enjoy belonging to and feeling part of a group and are able to collaborate, socialise and enjoy being with friends. It is in the Reception class that children start to develop preferences for friends and shared interests. They long to be accepted because they are developing a sense of personal identity and self-awareness. Yet, they also have a growing understanding of differences between themselves and others and the wonderful intuition to accept differences. However, this does not deter an eager 4-year-old from asking pertinent and sometimes insensitive questions of others who are different to themselves. This is because 4- and 5-year-olds are incredibly curious and have a thirst for knowledge. They can be really persistent in their questions and investigations if they want to understand or find something out.

By this age children are more able to listen and pay attention. They are developing empathy towards others and the ability to regulate their emotions. They are able to express their needs, explain, negotiate and argue their point of view.

At the same time, children of this age group are rapidly developing their physical and imagination skills. Physically, they are becoming more competent in terms of balance, strength, coordination and movement. They are refining their fine motor skills, developing pencil control and becoming more dexterous in using some tools safely and with control. They enjoy the outdoors where they can run, climb, chase, dance and experiment with movement and strength in different and sometimes risky ways. They manage their own personal hygiene and understand basic principles of staying healthy.

Their powers of imagination at this age are tremendous because they have the language now to be able to recall, retell and recreate stories. They have great memories for new facts and rules which supports their learning in mathematics and literacy. They enjoy telling you their own elaborate and sometimes long-winded tales of what they have experienced and they start to express their thoughts and ideas in creative ways using a range of media.

The implications of this for planning is that the children are now able to learn in a group context and will be able to benefit from short bursts of teacher-directed activities, in which skills are explicitly modelled and knowledge is shared. Examples of this would be shared reading and writing sessions, phonics and mathematics or topics, when children are taught as a whole class on the carpet, or PE lessons that take place in the formal context of the school hall. Circle times will also support the children to gain a sense of community and belonging and develop their growing awareness of diversity and social expectations. This teacher-directed and group-learning pedagogical approach to planning is underpinned by Vygotsky's and Bruner's socio-constructivist theory (Doherty and Hughes, 2014), in which children are provided with a scaffold to reach their next stage of development, known as their 'zone of proximal development' (ZPD). In this case the scaffold may be the knowledgeable adult who imparts knowledge or it may be the other children in the class, as they share their knowledge and ideas through social interaction during whole class teaching sessions.

Yet, in order to also meet children's desire for autonomy, support their rapid surge in physical development and their increasing imagination and creativity, it is clear that they also need to have plenty of time and opportunities for child-initiated learning. This tends to take place through uninterrupted time for play in the areas of continuous provision. This is the medium through which children can pursue their own interests and discover things for themselves, constructing their own knowledge and developing new skills through experimenting, making connections and exploring new possibilities. This type of learning is akin to Piaget's constructivist theory of learning (Garhart Mooney, 2000) and Bruner's spiral curriculum (Doherty and Hughes, 2014), in which children develop and learn through active, hands-on experimentation and have opportunities to revisit concepts, skills and knowledge and repeat experiences, so that they can consolidate, build upon and extend their learning.

TEACHING: WHAT ARE THE REQUIREMENTS OF THE EYFS STATUTORY FRAMEWORK?

The balance between planning for teacher-directed and child-initiated learning is supported and clearly articulated in the *Statutory Framework for the EYFS* (DfE, 2017, p9) which states that,

> *1.8. Each area of learning and development must be implemented through planned, purposeful play and through a mix of adult-led and child-initiated activity. Play is essential for children's development, building their confidence as they learn to explore, to think about problems, and relate to others. Children learn by leading their own play, and by taking part in play which is guided by adults. There is an ongoing judgement to be made by practitioners*

about the balance between activities led by children, and activities led or guided by adults. Practitioners must respond to each child's emerging needs and interests, guiding their development through warm, positive interaction. As children grow older, and as their development allows, it is expected that the balance will gradually shift towards more activities led by adults, to help children prepare for more formal learning, ready for Year 1.

The key word here is 'balance' and this is also backed up by Ofsted's definition of teaching which supports the notion that teachers must use their professional judgement when deciding on the balance between planning for free play and planning for direct teaching:

Teaching should not be taken to imply a 'top down' or formal way of working. It is a broad term which covers the many different ways in which adults help young children learn. It includes their interactions with children during planned and child-initiated play and activities: communicating and modelling language, showing, explaining, demonstrating, exploring ideas, encouraging, questioning, recalling, providing a narrative for what they are doing, facilitating and setting challenges. It takes account of the equipment they provide and the attention to the physical environment as well as the structure and routines of the day that establish expectations. Integral to teaching is how practitioners assess what children know, understand and can do as well as take account of their interests and dispositions to learning (characteristics of effective learning), and use this information to plan children's next steps in learning and monitor their progress.

(Ofsted, 2015)

✓ TIPS FOR PRACTICE

- Display a copy of Ofsted's definition of teaching in your setting, or take it into your placement setting and share it with the staff. It is a helpful reminder to all staff, senior managers and parents that all our interactions with children in all phases of the EYFS are examples of 'teaching'.

BRINGING IT ALL TOGETHER

Once you have established your pedagogical approach to planning, as discussed throughout this chapter (your balance between child-centred and outcomes-focused planning), you will be more prepared to be able to plan for a Reception class.

OBSERVATION

As with all age phases in the EYFS, your planning should be based on your assessment of what children need, based on their prior learning and attainment. This means observing the children, interacting with them and assessing their current stages of development and levels of attainment. There is a new statutory requirement to begin in the autumn of 2020 and which is currently being trialled, for Reception class teachers to carry out a baseline assessment of their children at the start of the year. It is important to note that the baseline assessment has been introduced to support the school accountability agenda and not to measure or track children's individual progress. It is intended to give the school a progress measure from attainment on entry to the end of Key Stage 2. Therefore, it will not be appropriate for Reception class teachers to use this to inform their planning for the children in their new class. Instead, they will need to use their observations of children and discussion with parents to understand children's interests and capabilities and to match their development to the milestones in *Development Matters* (Early Education, 2012), or similar documents outlining typical stages of child development.

PLANNING FOR THE LEARNING ENVIRONMENT

Planning for continuous provision in the Reception class should outline the progression of skills that children may achieve through playing independently in these areas. Bryce-Clegg (2013) provides detailed guidance on planning for continuous provision. He explains that continuous provision should not be viewed as provision that is continuously available to children, but that it is the provision for learning in the absence of an adult.

Table 10.3 Extract from a continuous provision plan outlining skills and ELGs

Role play area	Reception class
Progression of skills **(we are learning to …)**	**Early Learning Goals** **(this will support us to …)**
Listen to others Join in a conversation Sustain a conversation Imagine Act out a role Take turns Empathise Negotiate Lead the play Develop a story Explain and justify own opinions Dress independently Recreate known experiences Create imaginary experiences Represent thoughts and ideas through a range of media	• **Listening and attention:** listen attentively in a range of situations … give attention to what others say and respond appropriately, while engaged in another activity. • **Understanding:** follow instructions involving several ideas or actions … answer 'how' and 'why' questions about their experiences and in response to stories or events. • **Speaking:** children express themselves effectively, showing awareness of listeners' needs. They use past, present and future forms accurately when talking about events that have happened or are to happen in the future. They develop their own narratives and explanations by connecting ideas or events. • **Making relationships:** children play co-operatively, taking turns with others. They take account of one another's ideas about how to organise their activity. They show sensitivity to others' needs and feelings, and form positive relationships with adults and other children. • **People and communities:** children talk about past and present events in their own lives and in the lives of family members. They know that other children don't always enjoy the same things, and are sensitive to this. They know about similarities and differences between themselves and others, and among families, communities and traditions. • **Being imaginative:** children use what they have learnt about media and materials in original ways, thinking about uses and purposes. They represent their own ideas, thoughts and feelings through design and technology, art, music, dance, role-play and stories.

Many Reception classes have long-term provision plans displayed in each area of continuous provision. They should include within the plan a list of skills that children may develop through playing in that area of provision. Although child-centred in approach, this type of long-term planning may also include the specific ELGs that children will be supported to make progress towards if they are successfully developing the skills outlined in the plan. The example in Table 10.3 provides an extract from a more detailed continuous provision plan for the role play area. It shows the progression of skills to be developed in order to meet the longer-term outcomes.

MEDIUM-TERM PLANNING

In the Reception class medium-term planning is often used to cover planning for a block of two to six weeks, or a half term. It is useful for outlining the topics likely to be covered, enhancements to continuous provision and a summary of the key concepts, knowledge and understanding that you intend to teach. As this planning is covering a number of weeks and children learn in different ways and at different rates, it is not possible to outline the specific learning objectives in advance, week by week. These will depend on how children engage with the topic, the impact of unpredictable events and happenings within the class and will be different for different groups of children. However, it is a helpful organisational tool for the team to enable them to plan the learning environment in response to children's current interests and needs and to ensure there is appropriate coverage of knowledge, skills and understanding across all of the areas of learning. Table 10.4 provides an example of a medium-term plan in a Reception class. It starts with assessment of prior learning and identification of children's learning priorities. It is child-centred in its approach, allowing for flexibility to respond to individual needs, but it also provides some structure to enable the staff to gather resources, set up the environment and motivate to children to engage.

Table 10.4 Example of a medium-term plan in a Reception class

Assessment of prior learning	
What did the children achieve through the previous medium-term plan? *Based on observations of individual children and documented as required*	*Discuss with colleagues or reflect on your observations of children's learning over the past two weeks, what were their interests and what did they achieve? Identify any gaps in learning that need addressing. Keep notes of individual children who require extra support or challenge.*
What do they need to focus on next? *General whole class learning needs based on how they have engaged with and achieved through the previous medium-term plan* *Differentiated specific skills, e.g. for PD, reading, mathematics, writing are planned for and recorded on short-term planning*	Working collaboratively with peers Re-telling a story with prompts Answering how and why questions, using language to explain their thoughts Planning and designing their constructions Acting out a character role from a story How to measure accurately and compare lengths, Knowledge and use of mathematical vocabulary for shape, space and measure Knowledge and understanding of the local area

(Continued)

Table 10.4   (Continued)

Date: 15/03/19 (2–3 weeks)	Focus: Traditional tales	Core text: Three Little Pigs	Area of learning
Hook for learning:	New houses being built behind nursery play area. Children to go in groups to have a look, watch the builders at work, take photos, sketch the buildings, discuss what they see, start the class interest board: 'what do we want to find out?'		PSED C+L UW
Introduction:	Introduction to text through dialogic book talk Familiarise children with the story through signing the story, re-telling it and drawing a story map		C+L Literacy
PLODs: Possible Lines Of Development – focus on the skills, knowledge and understanding that you want children to develop. Choose a few possibilities and see how the children are responding. Be flexible and responsive to individual needs.	Exploring and experimenting with different materials for creating structures/den building Experimenting with cause and effect, forces, movement Empathy – understanding what it is like to feel afraid Self-regulation understanding and managing own emotions Story structures – story board sequencing, retelling stories with props, small world and puppets Mark making and writing – draw story maps, shared writing, write Movement and coordination – hiding, running, keeping still Using imagination to act out a character role		EAD Mathematics UW PSED Literacy Literacy PD EAD

Opportunities for child-initiated learning through Enhancements to Continuous Provision		
Role play Three Little Pigs home Story board, book and story props	**Outdoors** Design and construct: den building resource boxes	**Outdoor sand** Real bricks, sand and water mixing, tools and transporters, hard hats, hi-vis jackets
Construction Resourced as a building site, pictures of houses, non-fiction books, photos of locality	**Creative workshop** Range of materials for making a strong house	**Water** Movement: straws, tubing, wheel, materials for making sails
Evaluation/Observation notes:		

SHORT-TERM PLANNING

Short-term planning in the Reception class often takes the form of a weekly plan which is annotated daily to show how the teacher is reflecting on children's learning from day to day and adapting the provision and teaching to meet the children's needs. Some schools like to have a separate weekly plan for literacy, phonics and mathematics, outlining specific learning objectives for the whole class and breaking these down into more specific objectives for groups and individuals.

Others prefer a weekly overview of all areas of learning in one sheet and organised according to the daily routine of the class. This approach views every moment as a learning moment. It breaks the day into chunks of time and shows how the provision is organised to support learning through either child-initiated or teacher-directed learning. There is less detailed recording of learning objectives and more focus on adult roles and opportunities for child-initiated learning.

Table 10.5 is an extract from a weekly plan devised by Dawn Trucca, an EYFS leader of a Nursery and Reception class with four practitioners. Dawn uses a child-centred approach to planning. Her weekly plan shows how adults are deployed to support children to follow their own interests, while still providing a structure for teacher-directed and teacher-guided learning. The extract shows the morning sessions. The afternoon sessions follow the same pattern but with a focus on mathematics. Table 10.6 is another part of the weekly plan, showing Dawn's planning for the teacher-directed learning in literacy and the enhancements to the continuous provision that are planned to support child-initiated learning.

IN THE MOMENT PLANNING

Anna Ephgrave (2018) provides detailed guidance on how she has developed 'in the moment' planning in her Reception class with fantastic results in terms of children's achievement and end of year attainment levels. This type of planning is not all written down in advance; it combines long-, medium- and short-term planning through a forecast of predictable events and organisational considerations throughout the year. Its starting point is the planning of a safe and stimulating learning environment to support child-initiated learning. It requires skilled adults who know how to observe and tune into children's thoughts and interests. They reflect 'in the moment' on their observations of children, assessing their needs and tuning into their interests. Then they respond sensitively (using many of the strategies described in Ofsted's definition of teaching), to support, challenge and extend children's learning. Teaching in this context is successful because the adults are going through the planning cycle of observing, reflecting and responding in the moment that children are ready to make progress. So, they are able to capitalise on learning opportunities immediately as they happen, rather than having to record them on an observation form and then outline the next steps on the weekly plan. Children's learning and the teaching that has taken place is still recorded by teachers, but not in advance, as we have been used to doing traditionally. The recording of 'in the moment planning' is done after the event and becomes a record of the child's learning journey. For detailed information on this approach, which is completely child-centred, you are advised to look at Anna Ephgrave's work signposted at the end of this chapter in the suggestions for further reading.

Table 10.5 Extract from a weekly plan for a Nursery and Reception class, provided by Dawn Trucca, EYFS leader

Week beginning:		Weekly Planner Reception			
Reflections:					
Reflect on previous week's adult focused, child initiated, any significant observation and any feedback from parents/carers					
Pupil Premium – need to identify children and any additional intervention (support and challenge) that children receive each day/week					
Intervention Groups – which children and which intervention groups? (write initials of children in each intervention group that is planned)					
PSED intervention		**Reading interventions**			
C+L intervention		**Physical Dev intervention**			
Writing intervention		**Maths intervention**			

	Monday	Tuesday	Wednesday	Thursday	Friday
8.50–9.45	Individual read – staff name	Individual read – staff	Individual read – staff	Individual read – staff	Individual read – staff
Meet and Greet Continuous provision	Physical development intervention – staff	Physical development intervention – staff	Physical development intervention – staff	Physical development intervention – staff	Physical development intervention – staff
Literacy session 9.45–10.05	Re-introduce the book of the week	Learning intentions linked to focused text…	Learning intentions linked to focused text…	Shared writing	Shared writing
Teacher directed/ Continuous provision 10–11.00 Indoors/outdoors	Outdoor – staff Targeter (observations) staff Continuous provision Manager – staff Writing focus – staff	Outdoor – staff Targeter (observations) staff Continuous provision Manager – staff Writing focus – staff	Outdoor – staff Targeter (observations) staff Continuous provision Manager – staff Writing focus – staff	Outdoor – staff Targeter (observations) staff Continuous Provision Manager – staff Writing focus – staff	Outdoor – staff Targeter (observations) staff Continuous provision Manager – staff Writing focus – staff
Phonics/handwriting 11.00–11.25	(See separate planning for differentiated phase)	(See separate planning for differentiated phase)	(See separate planning for differentiated phase)	(See separate planning for differentiated phase)	(See separate planning for differentiated phase)
Circle time and guided read 11.30–11:50	**Story time – staff x2** **staff (1 group)** **staff (1 group)**	**Story time – staff x2** **staff (1 group)** **staff (1 group)**	**Story time – staff x2** **staff (1 group)** **staff (1 group)**	**Story time – staff x2** **staff (1 group)** **staff (1 group)**	**Story time – staff x2** **staff (1 group)** **staff (1 group)**

Table 10.6 Extract from weekly plan for teacher-directed tasks and child-initiated opportunities for learning, provided by Dawn Trucca, EYFS leader

Literacy focused activities	Area of learning targeted	Learning objective	Activities/Resources/Key questions/Vocabulary	Organisation/When/Where/How
Shared writing – I can apply my phonic knowledge and facts about the fish we have been learning about	Literacy: Writing	*I can hold my pencil correctly *I can use my phonic knowledge (phase 2 and phase 3) *I can write my name *I can form letters correctly	Writing frame, sound mat	Writing area every day – writing area – see above timetable
Guided reading	Literacy: Reading	*I can handle books correctly *I can begin to recognise key words *I can apply my phonic knowledge	Guided reading books Key words/characters	Quiet room and space in corridor – see above planner
Maths focused activities	Area of learning targeted	Learning objective	Activities/Resources/Key questions/Vocabulary	Organisation/When/Where/How
n/a this week (observation and assessment focus)				
PSE focused activities	Area of learning targeted	Learning objective	Activities/Resources/Key questions/Vocabulary	Organisation/When/Where/How
Self-confidence/making relationships	Self-confidence/making relationships	Initiates conversations, attends to and takes account of what others say	Snack chat, maths games, peg board game	In provision pm – see above planner
Continuous provision enhancements	Area of learning targeted	Learning objective	Activities/Resources/Key questions/Vocabulary	Organisation/When/Where/How
Size ordering	M:SSM	I can order the pictures	Fish pictures, scissors, glue	Maths area
Number formation	M/PD	I can form my numbers correctly	Worksheet, pencils	Maths area
Boat racing	PD EAD	I can design and make a boat/submarine/rafts	Boats, straws	Water area
Make a boat	ICT	I can choose and use a program	Wooden blocks	Construction area (indoor and outdoor)
iPads	EAD/PD/L	I can make my own booklet	iPads	Reading area
Under the sea paintings	UW/L		Paint, paper, paintbrushes	Painting area
Make fact book about fish			Booklet	Writing area

CONCLUSION

This chapter has discussed the challenges of Reception class planning for child-centred learning and identified a tension between two contrasting pedagogical approaches that influence Reception class practice. It has examined the end of year attainment outcomes (the ELGs) and considered how the benchmark of the GLD impacts Reception class teachers' decisions when planning for learning. An underlying message running through the chapter is the need for you to keep in mind how 4- and 5-year-olds learn when planning in the Reception class. Be sure to take account of their wealth of prior knowledge, their home experiences and unique capabilities. The EYFS statutory framework and Ofsted's definition of teaching will support you to articulate your pedagogical stance. The challenges of planning for child-centred learning within an outcomes-focused educational climate are difficult, but not insurmountable. Therefore, be confident to plan holistically across all areas of learning and development, in accordance with the principles of the EYFS, to develop children's dispositions to learning and to set them up for sustained lifelong learning.

FURTHER READING

Bryce-Clegg, A (2013) *Continuous Provision in the Early Years*. London: Bloomsbury.

Ephgrave, A (2012) *The Reception Year in Action: A Month by Month Guide to Success in the Classroom*. London: Routledge.

Jarvis, P, George, J, Holland, W and Doherty, J (2016) *The Complete Companion for Teaching and Leading Practice in the Early Years* (3rd edn). London: Routledge.

REFERENCES

Bronfenbrenner, U (1979) *The Ecology of Human Development*. Cambridge, MA: Harvard University Press.

Bryce-Clegg, A (2013) *Continuous Provision in the Early Years*. London: Bloomsbury.

Communication Council (2015) *The Links between Children and Young People's Speech, Language and Communication Needs and Social Disadvantage*, briefing paper. Available at www.thecommunicationtrust.org.uk/media/381242/the_links_between_children_and_yp_s_slcn_and_social_disadvantage_final.pdf (accessed 19 February 2018).

Department for Education (2017) *Statutory Framework for the Early Years Foundation Stage: Setting the Standards for Learning, Development and Care for Children from Birth to Five*. London: DfE.

Doherty, J and Hughes, M (2014) *Child Development Theory and Practice 0–11* (2nd edn). Harlow: Pearson Education.

Early Education (2012) *Development Matters in the Early Years Foundation Stage (EYFS)*. London: Early Education. Available at https://www.foundationyears.org.uk/wp-content/uploads/2012/03/Development-Matters-FINAL-PRINT-AMENDED.pdf

Ephgrave, A (2018) *Planning in the Moment with Young Children: A Practical Guide for Early Years Practitioners and Parents*. London: Routledge.

Garhart Mooney, C (2000) *Theories of Childhood: An Introduction to Dewey, Montessori, Erikson, Piaget and Vygotsky*. St Paul, MN: Redleaf Press.

McClelland, M and Wanless, S (2015) Introduction to the special issue: Self-regulation across different cultural contexts. *Early Education and Development*, *26*(5–6): 609–14.

McDowall Clark, R (2017) *Exploring the Contexts for Early Learning: Changing the School Readiness Agenda*. London: Routledge.

Murray, J (2015) Early childhood pedagogies: Spaces for young children to flourish. *Early Child Development and Care*, *185*(11–12): 1715–32.

Ofsted, June 2015 *Early Years Inspection Handbook*. Available at: www.gov.uk/government/publications/early-years-inspection-handbook-from-september-2015 (accessed 19 February 2018).

Roberts-Holmes, G (2015) The 'datafication' of early years pedagogy: 'If the teaching is good, the data should be good and if there's bad teaching, there is bad data'. *Journal of Education Policy*, *30*(3): 302–15.

SECTION 4

ENSURING QUALITY AND OUTCOMES

11 MONITORING AND EVALUATING EYFS PLANNING

Jo McEvoy

CHAPTER AIMS

By the end of this chapter you will be able to:

- identify the different layers of planning for children's learning in the EYFS
- explain why it is important to monitor and evaluate the impact of planning for children's learning and development
- develop your understanding of the role of the EYFS leader in ensuring quality provision and positive learning outcomes for all children through child-centred EYFS planning

INTRODUCTION

This final chapter will consider the role of the EYFS leader in monitoring and evaluating the effectiveness of planning for children's learning. It will begin by examining different layers of curriculum planning in the EYFS. This will be followed by an explanation of the terms 'monitoring' and 'evaluating', so that leaders are clear about the purpose and usefulness of quality, assuring the effectiveness of planning. Several practical examples of how to monitor and evaluate planning will be shared from different practitioner perspectives and a monitoring tool will be provided to support leaders in getting started on devising their own way of quality assuring the effectiveness of the planning in their setting.

In the preceding chapters of this book we have introduced practical suggestions for child-centred planning in the EYFS with underpinning theory and research. There have been consistent messages regarding the need for a holistic and flexible approach to planning which involves starting with observing and tuning into the needs and interests of individual children, then responding through your interactions and providing suitable resources or experiences to enable children to develop and learn and to grow in confidence and self-esteem. Different ways of planning have been presented from current practitioners in Early Years settings. Some have shared their experiences through case studies and interviews and others have shared their own samples of planning and formats that they have developed to suit their particular setting. What is clear from the diverse range of planning that is included is that there is no one way to plan for learning and development in the EYFS.

Therefore, it can be challenging for the EYFS leader to know how to monitor and evaluate the effectiveness of planning and its impact on children's learning and development. It is understood that the EYFS leader will already have underpinning knowledge and understanding of child development and the EYFS to draw on, but a good starting point is to be clear on the purpose of child-centred planning and the different layers of curriculum planning that support high quality provision and positive outcomes for children.

DIFFERENT LAYERS OF CURRICULUM PLANNING IN THE EYFS

In the EYFS, the term 'curriculum' encompasses all that the children experience from entering into our care at the start of the day. In essence, it is everything we do for children, which is depicted as 'Positive Relationships' in the EYFS framework (DfE, 2017) and everything we provide for them, depicted as 'Enabling Environments'. The EYFS promotes a view of childhood in which children are capable and competent learners (Unique Child). It draws on the socio-constructivist learning theories of Piaget, Vygotsky and Bruner (Doherty and Hughes, 2014) that propose a child-centred approach to learning through exploration, play and social interaction with peers and adults. In addition, it draws on the socio-cultural theories of Bronfenbrenner, Bandura and Rogoff (Doherty and Hughes, 2014) who highlight the deep and lasting influence of children's cultural traditions and family relationships, celebrating diversity and the wealth of learning opportunities this brings to our settings. It is for these reasons that a child-centred approach to planning for children's learning is proposed in the EYFS. Child-centred planning is that which takes account of the individual needs and interests of each child and responds sensitively with provocations, interactions and stimuli to ignite curiosity, motivate involvement and sustain engagement.

When monitoring and evaluating the effectiveness of EYFS planning it is helpful to consider three layers of the EYFS curriculum:

- child-initiated learning;
- adult-guided learning;
- adult-directed learning.

CHILD-INITIATED LEARNING

This layer of the curriculum forms the foundation for all that follows because it is the layer in which the potential for children's learning is at its greatest. It is concerned with how we provide opportunities for children to initiate and lead their own learning through play and exploration. It involves creating and maintaining a safe and stimulating physical environment indoors and out, often referred to as the 'continuous provision'. Continuous provision is made up of the different areas within the room and outside, in which children can select resources and play freely. For example, most settings will have a role play area, a book corner, a workshop or creative area, sand and water play areas, construction and small world areas. These are called 'areas of continuous provision' or 'permanent provision', since they are continually accessible to children and are permanent, in the sense that the resources are a permanent feature of the provision in the same way as the furniture and fittings in the room. This provides children with continuity and predictability, which fosters feelings of security and homeliness. By having continuous access to the resources, children are able to practise and refine their skills, returning to the same resources frequently, which supports them to make connections and build on and extend their prior learning. Such provision, though, requires thoughtful planning and resourcing. It is not possible to plan in advance for child-initiated learning, stating the learning objectives and outcomes that individual children will achieve, because we do not know how each child will utilise the area and each child has their own interests and individual stage of on-going development across one or more areas of learning. However, by planning the resources and thinking of the possibilities for play and learning, we are able to state broad learning possibilities based on typical stages of development across the seven areas of learning in the EYFS. In addition, we can consider how each area of continuous provision may potentially support children to develop positive dispositions to learning as outlined in the EYFS as the 'Characteristics of Effective Learning' (DfE, 2017). For example, Table 11.1 shows a plan for the sand area in a Nursery setting, demonstrating that the practitioners have thought carefully about the types of resources they have provided and the possibilities for children to learn and develop across all areas of the EYFS. Their starting point was to consider 'What will children do in this area?' and then to ask the question, 'So, what might they learn from this?' followed by, 'How can we help, support and extend their learning?' This is a fairly simple format for planning, but it gives a structure for monitoring and evaluating the extent to which the area of continuous provision does the job it sets out to do, that of supporting and extending children's learning through child-initiated activity. By observing the children at play in this area the EYFS leader will be able to ascertain the extent to which the resources and the adult interactions support children to achieve and also to identify where there are missed opportunities that can be rectified through alternative resources or different types of adult interactions.

ADULT-GUIDED LEARNING

This layer of the curriculum is the in-between part, a bridge between child-initiated learning and adult-directed learning. It is concerned with planning in response to children's interests and planning for predictable events or traditions and celebrations throughout the year. Examples of planning for this layer of the curriculum would include enhancements to the areas of continuous provision, based on children's interests, and planning focus activities that are accessible for any child to engage in with an adult around to support and follow the child's lead. For example, following children's interest in wild animals we might plan to temporarily enhance the creative workshop area with a box of different patterned fabrics and wall papers for children to explore, along with pictures of wild animals. A focus activity might involve supporting children to develop their communication, language and social skills through engaging in role play outside, going on a safari adventure, looking for toy animals. The practitioners may plan broadly for possible learning outcomes, but they will not be able to plan specific learning objectives for the many children who will access the focus activity and gain many different skills and aspects of knowledge from following their own interests in the safari adventure play. This type of planning also requires practitioners to plan in the moment, responding to what individual children say and do, with comments, suggestions and sometimes providing additional resources to extend their play. The EYFS leader will be able to monitor and evaluate the effectiveness of the focus activity through scrutiny of the written plan, including any evaluations of it or direct observation of the activity as it takes place (Table 11.2).

Table 11.1 Sample plan for sand area (child initiated learning)

Area of provision:	Dry sand area	Age range:	2–4 years

What will children do?	Area of learning	Key learning opportunities
Pour, dig, scoop	PD	Use simple tools effectively (PD)
Cover and bury objects	PD	Begin to take account of the needs of others
Fill, empty, compare, contrast	Mathematics	Take turns/share resources sometimes with support (PSED)
Make marks	PD, Literacy	Listen and respond to ideas expressed by others in conversation (C+L)
Talk about what they are doing	C+L	Use talk to connect ideas, explain what is happening (C+L)
Notice things, make comments, think, ask questions	UW	Count objects (M)
Play alongside others	PSED	Uses language of 'more' and 'fewer' to compare two sets of objects (M)
Make up stories and events, imaginative play	Literacy, EAD	Use everyday language to talk about size, weight, capacity (M)
		Recognise, create and describe patterns (M)
		Look closely at similarities, differences, patterns and change (UW)

Permanent resources	Role of the adult	Key vocabulary
Buckets and containers of different sizes	Play alongside	Full, empty, overflowing
Spades, different sizes	Ask open questions	Pour, scoop, dig
Scoops, spoons, different sizes	Narrate what they are doing	More, less,
Rake	Model vocabulary	Long, short, round, zig-zag
Sieve, collander	Observe and listen and note	
Straws, twigs and lolly sticks	Make suggestions, what if? … make comments	
Small tubs of stones, pebbles, shells, other natural materials	Support turn taking and co-operative play	
Small tubs of small world resources: people, vehicles, dinosaurs, animals	Follow children's lead	
Water wheel		

How will you know that children are learning? (Assessment strategies)	
Look for:	Listen for:
<ul><li>children's levels of involvement and engagement</li><li>how children handle equipment – fine motor skills</li><li>the choices children make in their play – interests and schemas</li><li>children being able to share, take turns, play collaboratively</li><li>what motivates and excites the children</li><li>how children communicate without speaking</li></ul>	<ul><li>how children explain or narrate what they are doing</li><li>how children engage in conversations</li><li>what mathematical vocabulary children use</li><li>questions children ask</li><li>children's comments and answers</li><li>the structure and content of children's language, the vocabulary they use</li></ul>

Table 11.2 Sample plan for focus activity (adult guided learning)

Rationale/Prior learning	Children: Any children who wish to join in
Three children in the class visited the safari park together with their families. They have shared their experience with the class through 'show and tell'. The children have watched a video clip of the safari park and this has sparked an interest in learning about wild animals	**Age:** 3–5 years **Date:** 15–17 June (during continuous provision time outdoors, morning and afternoon). Adult to guide and support for three days then leave out as child-initiated activity for as long as children remain interested in it

Activity	Learning intentions	Areas of learning	Role of adult	Resources
Play safari park adventure outside with the children. Use of Little Tikes cars and cardboard box self-made vehicles. Entrance kiosk (tickets, till and money) set up near woodland space. Pictures of animals and toy animals placed around the woodland area. Animal masks available for children to act out being the animals. Set up cleaning and feeding area with dressing up clothes for animal carers.	To enjoy role play as part of a group To recreate and act out a role To negotiate with others, make suggestions and taking account of others' views, needs and wants To move in creative ways to represent animal movements and negotiate space To recognise, name and describe different animals Develop breadth of vocabulary relating to wild animals and habitats Use numbers in role play Count, add and subtract using coins (1p, 2p, 5p and 10p)	PSED EAL, C+L PSED, C+L PD UW UW, C+L MD	Play alongside children, observe and respond to their contributions. Support turn taking, negotiating and imagination. Model how to serve at the entrance kiosk, counting out money, writing out tickets, giving instructions of where to go in the park. Model different roles to play – guest, animal, animal carer. Introduce and frequently model new vocabulary – animal names and descriptive words, mathematical vocabulary, directions and positional vocabulary.	Several trikes and cardboard boxes for making vehicles Dressing up clothes Binoculars Mark-making resources Bag of coins (1ps, 2ps and 5ps) Till Toy animals Animal masks and range of fabric lengths Mops, buckets, brushes and cloths for cleaning Containers for animal 'food' Large blocks for making animal enclosures
How will you know that learning is taking place? What will children be able to do, know, understand?	Play in a group taking turns with the resources Listen to each other and take turns in the conversations Make suggestions about what to do and how to proceed in their play Use their imagination to act out a role of a person or an animal Name some of the animals correctly and use some appropriate vocabulary to describe them Understand that animals need us to care for them and respect them because they can also be dangerous Negotiate space using a trike, balance bike or toy car Create their own vehicle using cardboard boxes and other craft resources Create enclosures using large blocks and planks Solve problems and persevere when creating and constructing Develop self-confidence through negotiating with others and making suggestions Count pennies to 10 Recognise numbers 1,2, 5 and 10 and understand that 2p, 5p and 10p equal the equivalent number of pennies (2, 5, 10) Begin to add small numbers using money (1p, 2p, 5p and 10p coins) Use mark making and writing for a purpose (signs, labels) Use their phonic knowledge to write some words that can be read by others Know what a safari park is and what happens there			

ADULT-DIRECTED LEARNING

This layer of the curriculum is concerned with the times when the adult plans to teach a specific skill or aspect of knowledge to a specific group of children at a specific time. It is planned in advance and most frequently used with older children who are able to maintain attention. Examples of this type of planning are when we gather children together on the carpet to teach a literacy session, phonics, mathematics or topic. Additionally, we may work with a small group of children on a guided reading or small group maths topic, or with one or two children at a time on an intervention teaching activity. These adult-directed sessions, like child-initiated and adult-guided, may too be play based, fun and interactive. However, the difference between these layers of the curriculum is that this layer is fully directed and led by the adult, who has a particular objective in mind, whereas the child-initiated layer is fully directed and led by the child and the adult has to ascertain the child's particular objective through observation, participation and sensitive interaction. There are examples of this type of planning in the previous chapters.

REFLECTION ACTIVITY 11.1

Can you identify in your workplace or in your placement setting how each of these three layers of the curriculum is planned for and implemented?

How might it be useful for the EYFS leader to use these three layers of the curriculum to monitor and evaluate the effectiveness of planning?

MONITORING AND EVALUATING

It is the responsibility of the EYFS leader to ensure that all children are given equal opportunities to be able to reach their potential. This requires the leader to continually monitor and evaluate the quality of the practice and the provision, which therefore includes scrutiny of how the practitioners are planning for children's learning. The two terms 'monitoring' and 'evaluating' may be perceived by some practitioners as threatening if they feel that monitoring is something that is done to them or 'on' them and then leads to a judgement of their practice that may require improvement. This will inevitably involve more work and can become a negative experience. Therefore, it is important to be clear at the outset about what is understood by the terms 'monitoring' and 'evaluating' and what their purpose is. As a student, you will not yet be in a position to monitor and evaluate the planning in your setting, but you will be continually monitoring and evaluating your own planning and considering the practice of more experienced practitioners and your mentor. To develop your understanding, it might be helpful for you to liken the processes of monitoring and evaluating to the reflective process, whereby you focus your attention on an aspect of practice to understand it more clearly, so that future practice might be more effective. For this is exactly what the process of monitoring and evaluating helps the EYFS to achieve.

REFLECTION ACTIVITY 11.2

What do these terms mean to you?

Monitoring is …
Evaluating is …

Why do you think it is necessary to monitor and evaluate practice and why do you think some practitioners may feel threatened by the process?

THE QUALITY IMPROVEMENT PROCESS

The actions of monitoring and evaluating are an integral part of the quality improvement process. Continuous quality improvement is necessary first and foremost for accountability purposes. At the heart of our practice we are accountable to the children in our care. Every child is entitled to high quality care and early education, no matter where they come from or who their parents/carers are. One of the main purposes of the EYFS statutory framework is to ensure equality of opportunity for all children from birth to 5 years of age (DfE, 2017). In addition, though, we are accountable to the parents and carers who place their trust in us to care for their children. They should expect the best for their children and feel secure that we are planning in response to their children's needs and interests. On a wider scale, we are also accountable to our employers and to all who contribute to the funding of statutory childcare and education through the government's Department for Education. There are also many other reasons for quality improvement that are equally important, but not always acknowledged. Consider the following list and tick off the reasons that are important to you:

- accountability;
- sustainability, making sure the setting will attract business;
- keeping abreast with current evidence based practices;
- identifying and celebrating achievement;
- identifying and responding to gaps in provision;
- supporting team involvement in a common goal;
- personal and professional fulfilment;
- ethical practice.

When everyone involved in the quality improvement process is clear about the reasons for monitoring and evaluating, the process becomes a genuine and collaborative task, but it is also important to establish a common understanding of what monitoring and evaluation entails.

MONITORING

Monitoring, as part of the quality improvement process, is generally understood as a form of checking; checking that something is happening, finding out what is going on, seeing if what has been developed and agreed as quality practice is still being maintained. This may be why some people find it a negative concept, one in which there is a perceived lack of trust, suggesting that we have to be checked up on. A more helpful way of understanding this term may be to think of it as 'collecting the evidence' (Edgington, 2005). Monitoring is a way of proactively looking for the evidence of what we do. For example, when the EYFS leader monitors the planning they may look for evidence of clear learning objectives, coverage of the seven areas of learning, frequency of planning and many other aspects too. What monitoring does not do, however, is to evaluate the relevance or the effectiveness of the learning objectives or the other aspects under scrutiny. This is where 'evaluation' is used.

EVALUATING

Evaluating, as part of the quality improvement process, is about making judgements against an agreed criterion (Edgington, 2005). This part of the process is the most crucial and requires the leader to have sound professional judgement and values, based on critical understanding of child development, the EYFS and the setting's own policies and agreed values. Evaluation is the place where impact is considered and a judgement is made on the extent to which the impact is effective. For example, when the EYFS leader evaluates the effectiveness of the planning they will need to consider many sources of evidence in addition to the actual planning documents in order to ascertain whether children are achieving their potential. The monitoring tool at the end of this chapter provides some examples of how to do this (see Table 11.4).

HOW DO EYFS LEADERS MONITOR AND EVALUATE PLANNING?

The following case studies are shared by current EYFS leaders in different settings. Each describes how they monitor and evaluate the effectiveness of the planning in their setting. Can you identify where they are monitoring (collecting the evidence) and where they are evaluating (making the judgement against agreed criteria)?

CASE STUDY 11.1

Miriam

Miriam is an Early Years Teacher (EYTS) and the EYFS leader in a primary school. She currently teaches the reception class.

On a daily basis I evaluate my 'lessons' and make notes as to what went well, what didn't and if the children enjoyed and responded well to the activity. I reflect on the outcomes and if/how they met the learning intention. On a termly basis I monitor the children's progress and I highlight areas of learning in which children have made more than expected progress. I evaluate how this has been achieved – identifying whether it is due to any specific planning, activities or particular opportunities I have provided for them. Likewise, for any areas in which children have not made expected progress I evaluate the opportunities/activities and planned lessons that may have contributed to the lack of progress, along with other factors, e.g. attendance/behaviour. The usual assessments of maths/phonics/reading/writing help to highlight areas that need further input and this informs subsequent planning. At the end of the year I review my long-term plan and highlight areas that may need more attention. For example, with my cohort last year, the assessment data showed that Literacy was an area for improvement because a number of children just missed out in reaching the Good Level of Development (GLD) because they did not achieve the Early Learning Goal for writing. Therefore, this year I have implemented 'movement for learning' sessions for a group of children still developing their mark making skills, along with other specific pre literacy based activities in the autumn term. Monitoring of the observations is also done regularly to ensure that all areas of learning are covered. I have found there is always a heavy emphasis on literacy and maths (I know this should not happen!) and sometimes the other areas such as Understanding the World and Expressive Arts and Design are neglected and not given sufficient time. Through monitoring, I was alerted to this and I then amended my timetable to allow more time for these areas of learning and planned specifically for them. We did some fabulous work around Andy Goldsworthy last year which may not have happened without it being planned into the weekly sessions. I find I am constantly monitoring and evaluating everything we do, all the time. I don't always record this monitoring, it can be quite 'fluid' in that it changes and moves with the children throughout the year. However, the cycle of plan/do/review is what underpins my monitoring and evaluation of planning and being reflective is what helps me to do it.

CASE STUDY 11.2

Melissa

Melissa is an Early Years Teacher (EYTS) and the manager of a private day Nursery caring for babies, toddlers and young children to the age of 5.

All of our planning starts with observing the children. We in-put our observations onto an iPad and make links to the EYFS areas of learning. So, staff complete observations of their children and make their EYFS links. They also write 'next steps' following on from that observation, which is, in effect, their planning. They add this to the weekly planning sheet. I monitor the planning sheets every week to ensure learning intentions are clear and appropriate. This is an area we have been working on recently and there has been an improvement now in focussing on the learning intentions for children to achieve, rather than just planning for activities to take place in the different areas of the room. I then observe staff carrying out what they have planned to do, so that I can see if the learning intentions are met by the children. I differentiate how I monitor the planning for different staff according to their level of knowledge and experience. For example, with a less experienced member of staff or a staff member whose practice needs to improve, I will ask them to do a detailed activity plan so that we can identify exactly where they are struggling to meet children's needs. I can then support them through 360 degree peer observations in which staff observe me as manager and observe other staff who are confident in delivering their planned activity well, which offers a good opportunity for reflecting on the quality of teaching and how to document the children's learning. Staff are planning a lot better now for individual children, which is seen in the observations of practice and in children's progress records.

COLLECTING THE EVIDENCE AND EVALUATING THE IMPACT

From the case studies, it is apparent that monitoring and evaluating planning requires much more than simply scrutinising written plans. The EYFS leader needs to consider many different sources of evidence to see whether the planning is having an impact on children's learning, development and well-being. Monitoring involves collecting and collating evidence of how and what is being planned, whilst evaluating is concerned with judging how effective it is. Sources of evidence that will help you to evaluate how effective the planning is will include a wider range of evidence than the actual written plans, such as:

- direct observation of learning and teaching;
- practitioners' own evaluations of their planning and teaching;
- spot checks on room organisation and routines;
- children's records (observations of their learning, contributions from parents/carers);
- regular checking of tracking data – individuals, groups and cohorts;
- minutes or observations of planning and team meetings;
- chatting with practitioners, children and parents/carers.

When evaluating the effectiveness of planning the EYFS leader should consider the following areas:

1. coverage;
2. content;
3. impact.

Coverage:

- Is there a balance of planning to support child-initiated, adult-guided and adult-directed learning?
- Are all areas of learning and development (DfE, 2017) addressed frequently and adequately?
- Are the Characteristics of Effective Learning (DfE, 2017) considered and actively promoted?

Content:

- Is planning based on children's needs and prior learning?
- Is the daily routine planned to allow children sufficient time to engage in child-initiated activity and with adults available to support?
- Is there planning in place for regular enhancements to the continuous provision?
- Does planning for focus activities support the relevant areas of learning and development in the EYFS and the Characteristics of Effective Learning?
- If learning objectives and success criteria are written in advance, is it clear what children are intended to learn and what the outcome of that might be?
- If planning is 'in the moment', are the responses of the adults suitably matched to the developmental stage of the children?
- Does planning consider all of the following elements:
  - o what the children may learn;
  - o how you will know they have been successful in learning;

- o   what the children may do;
- o   what adults may do;
- o   resources;
- o   how the adult will support children with atypical development.

Impact:

- Does planning result in all children making progress in their learning and development? (How do you know? What evidence supports your judgement?)
- What are the strengths of the planning systems in place? (How do you know? What evidence supports your judgement?)
- Where are the gaps in provision or adult interactions that are resulting in missed opportunities for children to make progress? (How do you know? What evidence supports your judgement?)

The whole purpose of monitoring and evaluating planning is that it leads to improvements, better outcomes for children and better staff motivation. Therefore, it is essential that through this process, areas for further development are identified and the steps required to address gaps are put in place. For example, some staff may require further training on how to observe and assess children's progress, or they may require further training on supporting children who are not making appropriate progress.

REFLECTION ACTIVITY 11.3

As a student or practitioner who is not yet the EYFS lead:

Take time to review the planning in your setting and consider each area in turn: content, coverage and impact. If possible, discuss how the planning is monitored and evaluated and review the evidence.

MONITORING AND EVALUATING THE PLANNING IN YOUR SETTING

The tool shown in Table 11.3 is intended to support EYFS leaders or EYFS teams to work together to develop their own ways of continuously reflecting on their planning processes to ensure maximum impact on children's development, learning and well-being. It has been designed to support you to monitor and evaluate the effectiveness of your planning. It may be filled in individually by practitioners to support self-evaluation and reflection, by teams to support collaborative quality improvement work, or by leaders to inform their overall quality improvement processes. The three broad areas, 'coverage, content and impact', provide a structure for the process and the questions are there as prompts to facilitate reflection and discussion. It is expected that you will add your own questions too. It is helpful to take time to complete the evidence boxes with your notes and evidence of 'how you know', because this supports a transparent and objective approach to whole team quality improvement. The evaluation boxes are intended to support you to identify priorities for development where there are gaps, or weaker areas that require attention. It is hoped that this tool will help to create a supportive and collaborative approach to developing and continuously improving the effectiveness of your planning so that all children make progress, are motivated and enjoy the experiences you provide for them. In Table 11.4 you will see an example of one section of the tool completed, which may help you to get started with your own audit. There is no prescriptive way of doing it, just as there is no one way of planning. It is hoped that this example will simply give you a stimulus to develop your own way of carrying out meaningful and genuine self-evaluation.

Table 11.3 Quality improvement audit for child-centred planning

Quality improvement audit for child-centred planning			
Aspects of planning	**Questions to consider**	**Evidence**	**Evaluation**
Coverage	How do we plan for all the areas of learning and development? How do we cover all of the aspects of each area of learning and development? How do we plan for the Characteristics of Effective Learning?		
Content	How do we use assessments to inform our planning? What is the balance of child-initiated and adult-initiated experiences? How do adults support and extend children's learning and development?		
Impact	How are children who are not making expected progress identified and supported? How is the children's progress monitored? How do we evaluate our teaching?		
Key areas for development: (identify up to three priorities for development and possible actions to achieve them)			

Table 11.4 Example section of audit tool: monitoring and evaluating the planning in your setting

Quality improvement audit for child-centred planning

Aspects of planning	Questions to consider	Evidence	Evaluation (What works well and why? Even better if?)
Coverage	How do we ensure our planning covers predictable events throughout the year and responds to unexpected events and interests of children? How do we plan for all the areas and aspects of learning and development? How do we plan for the Characteristics of Effective Learning (CoEL)?	*Long-term planning covers festivals and seasons.* *Overview of the year shows links to all 7 areas of learning and development.* *Short-term planning in baby room and toddlers has more focus on prime areas than specific. Short-term planning is done by key persons, they highlight which Areas of Learning and aspects have been covered.* *All planning (long, medium and short) No formal recording of where CoEL are planned for.* *Child Observations show most children are 'active learners' and are engaging in play and exploration' very little evidence of children thinking critically and creating'. There is no recorded evidence of planning for this characteristic of learning.* *Weekly timetables - pre-school room, children given long slots of time (1.5 hours) in continuous provision, less time in toddler room due to the routine of snacks, designated nappy changing time and lunch.* *Parent newsletter parents asked to contribute ie their cultural traditions, providing artefacts etc. evidence of this was observed in observations of practice and room spot checks.* *Parent noticeboard opportunity for parents to put up wow moments, most are dated from three months ago.*	Sufficient coverage of areas and aspects of learning throughout the year. Appropriate balance across the prime and specific areas to match the developmental stages of children. Short-term planning by key person needs monitoring regularly by room leaders to ensure there is coverage of all areas in all age ranges. Long-term planning is a strength, parents are involved and this promotes awareness of diversity and supports inclusion. Planning for the CoEL needs attention, particularly around Thinking Critically and Creating so that there are no missed opportunities for children to develop these skills and so that the adults are confident to promote them in practice. Staff respond well to children's interests in the moment, but these interests are not shared among staff, recorded or information regularly gained from parents. This may restrict the depth and breadth of children's learning because the learning potential sparked from interests is not fully exploited.

Key areas for development: (identify priorities for development and possible actions to achieve them)

1. To provide more opportunities to promote children's thinking and creativity skills
Actions:
*   Plan for one 'curiosity' activity each week through enhancements to continuous provision and additional resources
*   Peer observations for staff to provide feedback to each other on how they are prompting and extending children's thinking skills
*   Staff training on communication techniques to promote children's thinking skills (use of podcasts and literature)

2. To plan from children's interests more frequently and in more depth so that children are supported to make sustained progress and engage more in 'Active Learning' (CoEL):

*   Delegate staff member to monitor the Wow board and be proactive in getting parents to contribute more frequently
*   Target a few children each week for focus observations and build on their interests over several days
*   Introduce group planning time in pre-school room so that children are involved in planning what they want to learn – visit settings who are already doing this to observe how it works in practice

CONCLUSION

Just as there is no one way to plan for children's learning and development in the EYFS, it is clear that that there is also no single way to monitor and evaluate the effectiveness of the setting's planning. This is a complex task that requires consideration of much more evidence than scrutiny of written plans. Therefore, this chapter has outlined some general guidance and principles upon which EYFS leaders can develop their own ways of monitoring and evaluating the effectiveness of planning. A definition for monitoring and evaluation has been proposed, in which monitoring is concerned with seeking evidence that can demonstrate what is being done, while evaluation is about judging how effective it is. It has been established that monitoring and evaluation are an integral part of the quality improvement process, which may sometimes have negative connotations for some practitioners. The need to involve all stakeholders in the process has been emphasised and the importance of being clear from the outset about the purpose and process has been encouraged. It is hoped that the case studies and tips for practice included in this chapter will support you to evaluate your own planning and make further improvements to your practice.

FURTHER READING

Jarvis, P, George, J, Holland, W and Doherty, J (2016) *The Complete Companion for Teaching and Leading Practice in the Early Years* (3rd edn). London: Routledge.

Lindon, J, Lindon, L and Beckley, P (2016) *Leadership in Early Years*. London: Hodder Education.

Rodd, J (2015) *Leading Change in the Early Years: Principles and Practice*. Maidenhead: Open University Press.

REFERENCES

Department for Education (2017) *Statutory Framework for the Early Years Foundation Stage: Setting the Standards for Learning, Development and Care for Children from Birth to Five*. London: DfE.

Doherty, J and Hughes, M (2014) *Child Development Theory and Practice 0–11* (2nd edn). Harlow: Pearson Education.

Edgington, M (2004) *The Foundation Stage Teacher in Action: Teaching 3, 4 and 5 Year Olds* (3rd edn). London: Paul Chapman Publishing.

INDEX

Lightning Source UK Ltd.
Milton Keynes UK
UKHW052201231119
354110UK00009B/452/P